PERSECUTED, STATELESS, FREE

PERSECUTED, STATELESS, FREE

One girl's flight from the Nazis

LISA MAC VITTIE
WITH
DONALD W MAC VITTIE

ISBN: 1548716464
ISBN 13: 9781548716462
Library of Congress Control Number: 2017910805
CreateSpace Independent Publishing Platform
North Charleston, South Carolina

To the Survivors

There was much between there and here, and yet you persevered. You found your new home in one of the many countries that eventually took in refugees, and you thrived. Though our story starts in terror, it ends in joy and peace.

To Those Who Have Never Seen Terror

It is my sincere hope that you never see the type of persecution that the Nazis brought to a fever pitch. But if you do, this book is for you, to remind you that *this too shall pass*. Do all that you can to stop such oppression when it starts, but should you be the victim, there is hope; cling to it.

To the Hebrew International Aid Society (HIAS)

While governments avoided addressing the Jewish refugee problem, HIAS, among other organizations, stood up and offered help without asking for reward or recognition. They continue to offer this service across the globe today—and not only to Jewish refugees.

To the Chinese Citizens of Shanghai

We refugees struggled in many ways while living in Shanghai. Open hostility from the Chinese population would have made our struggles far worse. Though there was occasional friction, there was little outright hostility until toward the end of the revolution. Your patience and understanding may well have saved many of our lives.

The Authors

This is Lisa's story, as told to Donald.

CONTENTS

I DON'T KNOW WHAT TO SAY

What must I say?
I don't know how to write about what happened to her,
and what she experienced
When I do it will sound contrived
How can I write about that Earthly hell?
I can't, it will never do her justice
How can I write about her suffering? By smooth-
ing and slapping it into a rhyme?
Presenting it on beautiful paper, itching for a big gold star?
I cannot
I will not attempt to put salve on wounds
too deep for me to comprehend,
too wide for me to fathom
What can I say, as she describes chil-
dren in cattle trucks rolling away?
Rolling away over the hill and waving to their mothers,
What can I say?
What should I write?
Should I write that her experiences will never be forgotten,
that such hatred will never happen again?

But that would be a lie, wouldn't it?
Because it happens every day, every minute of every day, in every heart and mind,
Mine included
I can say all the words,
"There were showers of bedbugs
Dysentery,
Ghettos, camps and gas chambers"
But what does that do to me? Does it penetrate my heart at all?
Is it internalized? Can it be?
What do those words mean?
I don't know what to say except,
"Please God may I never feel that pain"
I don't know what to write or how to write it,
or even whether it should be written
I have no words
They slipped out from under me,
and crushed me with their heavy hollowness,
and bound my tongue and choked my heart,
Because in the face of this, this single harrowing experience out of millions of similar ones,
I am shocked into silence
I no longer know what to say.
Poem by Emily van Oudenhove,
courtesy of the Rodgers Center for Holocaust
Education at Chapman University.

Chapter 1

NATION AND FAMILY—A JEWISH FAMILY IN 1930S GERMANY

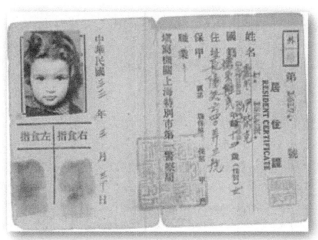

Lilly's Shanghai Residence Certificate

For all its problems, Berlin was a thriving city in the mid-1930s. It had museums, opera, zoos, playhouses, and an abundance of shops. Growing up in this environment, belonging to a family who today would be considered upper middle class, meant a childhood of joy. That is the world that Liselotte (Lilly) Isaack knew before the troubles started.

Lilly's family was well-off enough that they saw movies (still a novelty), went to the opera, and frequently visited both museums and zoos. Her father, Kurt Phillip Isaack, was a business manager who came from a wine-making family of wealth with a family history of serving in the German army. That side of the family was large, and family gatherings could be quite rambunctious. Kurt himself attended university in Heidelberg, and his brothers and sisters went to similarly storied educational institutions. They also happened to be Jewish, something that mattered a lot the more the 1930s rolled on. Lilly's mother, Elisabeth (Dietsch) Isaack, came from a shoemaker's family, who were well-off enough themselves. Her father supported the family well on his shoemaking, and that side of the family also had a history of patriotically serving Germany in her armed forces. Significantly this side of the family was not of Jewish heritage. Lilly was the youngest of three children. She was born in 1932, her sister Ingrid in 1931, and her brother Joachim (Joe) was born in 1926. When this story begins, Lilly was not yet old enough to attend school.

RISE OF THE NAZIS

When the Nazis were beginning to gain popularity in Germany, they promised the very things that other politicians more doused in the fabric of the status quo were afraid to promise. Germany was suffering under horrific war debts and restrictions under World War I's Versailles Treaty, combined with the prolonged impact of the Great Depression. The people of Germany wanted—you could even say *needed*—hope, and the National Socialist Party offered it. In modern times, it can be difficult to understand just exactly how popular the Nazis were, so by way of example, more than four thousand cities, towns, and villages made Adolph Hitler an honorary citizen in the early to mid-thirties, most of them before he was chancellor of Germany.

After a time and some rather crude violence, the choice started to clarify. The old parties would not retain control of Germany—or at least not remain dominant in that control—and the citizens of Germany were faced with a choice: communism or national socialism. They chose national socialism.

Lilly's family was there for these strange times. Her father, being Jewish, watched events unfold carefully as the Nazis started to show signs of anti-Semitism. Her mother, being from a Lutheran family, joined the National Socialist Party so that the family had a lever in official business, should things continue down the dark path of discrimination.

EVEN THE CHILDREN

Continue down a dark path they did. One day, Lilly's siblings did not return from school. Eventually Joachim made his way home to inform their parents that he and the other children of Jewish heritage had been removed from the public school and had been taken to a different location to attend private schools for Jewish children only. Lilly was too young to pay that much attention to others' feelings, but it does not take a large amount of imagination to envision her parents' horror upon hearing this news; her sister, Ingrid was only in kindergarten and was not home yet.

They spent the late afternoon and early evening tracking down where exactly Ingrid might be, finally learning which school she had been taken to and that she was still there, and then getting her home safe. That was the sign that things would continue to deteriorate for Jews in Germany. Soon, friends of the family, people whom Lilly had known her entire life, would not talk to them because they were Jewish. While there were other problems, large and small, as petty officials grew to understand that German Jews were not protected like other citizens, the final straw for the Isaack family came on Kristallnacht: November 8–9, 1938.

But first a bit of personal information that will play into this larger story. During this time of worsening conditions for Germany's Jewish citizens, in 1937, Lilly contracted polio. While largely defeated in the twenty-first century, polio was a horrific disease in the 1930s that killed many and left many others crippled. Lilly was placed in a sanatorium (hospital) for long-term care, and her right side from the hip down was placed in a plaster cast. This was a very serious development, treatment for the disease being rather basic at the time, as medicine was still learning what worked and what did not and inoculations were a thing of the future.

DECISION TIME

Over time, the government grew restrictive of Jewish rights, and one of the things restricted was travel. By limiting the days and hours that the offices granting travel permission were open, the authorities controlled exfiltration. After Kristallnacht, the Isaack family had a decision to make. They were a large family who had deep ties in Berlin and who had lived in Germany for generations. As with most families, what was to happen next was the subject of a significant amount of debate. Lilly's grandfather was adamant that things were not so dire that leaving Germany was imperative, while her father and uncle were certain things would get worse before improving.

The boys decided to leave, the grandfather to stay. Lilly's father and uncle took turns standing in line at the travel offices, waiting their turn to get permission to travel. The problem was that for the extended family, they needed more than just permission to leave Germany; they also needed visas, passage on a ship to somewhere, and cash to cover expenses outside of travel. Skirting the officials and traveling without permission, Kurt took a trip to Hamburg to visit a friend in the travel business and managed to acquire tickets for all of them on a Japanese liner named *Terukuni Maru* bound for Shanghai.

Shanghai was really the only option at that point in time for those seeking to leave Germany quickly. Most nations had a quota system, and applicants had to wait their turn to be called upon. With the pressure of many people trying to get out of Germany, most countries' quotas filled up quickly. Shanghai was an international port. By both treaty and convention, it was open to any who traveled there without the requirement of a visa. Considering that they were trying to get permission for nine people—the five members of Lilly's family, her uncle John and aunt Harriet, and her aunt's elderly father, Mr. Hermann Bondy—to leave Germany, their decision was probably a wise one. The authorities would have made all sorts of roadblocks and required taxes that amounted to their next year's salary after forfeiture of possessions. It is unlikely that they would have ever left by official channels.

SOMETIMES FLIGHT WAS FUTILE

Even leaving Germany was no guarantee of successfully getting away from the Nazis. On May 13, the German passenger liner *St. Louis* set sail from Hamburg, Germany, to Havana, Cuba. She left with permission of the German government, and most of her passengers were Jewish citizens fleeing the Nazi regime. Most of the passengers had been sold landing papers in Cuba to get ashore while they waited for US immigration to clear them to travel on to America. By 1939, the exodus of Jewish people from Europe had grown so large that very few countries were accepting Jewish immigrants. The United States had (and still has) a quota system that limited how many people from a given country were allowed to enter.

The quota for 1939 was full, and the people on the *St. Louis* were on the list but hoped to wait in Cuba for their turn to journey on to the United States. Before the ship left, Cuban authorities recognized that the Cuban director general of immigration had been selling landing passes for his own profit, and the president of Cuba canceled all landing passes he issued. The passengers of the *St. Louis* were not told. When the ship made port in Havana, all but a few passengers were refused entry into Cuba, and the ship sailed around Florida while using wireless to ask the US government for an exception to immigration law. The US president chose that between the existing law and the state of the union (still recovering from the Depression), there was nothing the United States could do for them. The ship was turned around and returned to Europe. Aid associations managed to get the refugees homes in other European countries. But most of those countries were later overrun, and those who had come so tantalizingly close to freedom became victims of the Holocaust after all.

Shanghai, by not requiring entry paper work, avoided such problems.

Thus the destination was more thrust upon the Isaacks (and nearly twenty thousand other European Jewish citizens) than decided upon, and yet it was a chance at freedom that could not be passed up. Some of the family, notably the grandparents, believed that the anti-Semitism running rampant in the country and sponsored by a hostile government was a temporary phase that would pass. But the two families, Lilly's family and that of her uncle, were unwilling to wait to see if it got better or worse.

The German authorities decided that Lilly, as a Jewish child with polio, was using too many resources required for good Aryan citizens; she was classified as an invalid and sent home from the hospital to her fate. The doctors did as they could for her before discharge, including giving Mrs. Isaack a strict diet based upon the best medical art at the time. The diet was purely vegetarian, as the belief was that polio was best treated with less red meat and more "healing" vegetables. They also made certain that Lilly's cast was set for her time at home, although it is unlikely they knew they were fashioning her a traveling cast.

Mrs. Isaack was a fastidious woman, and yet when Lilly returned home, the house was in disarray. Many of the furnishings and possessions of the Isaack family were missing, and those things that were still there were jumbled and being packed. To facilitate leaving Germany and to defeat the confiscatory policies of the Nazi regime—Jewish people leaving the country had to leave behind all their possessions—she had arranged to ship most of their belongings on a slow ship to China. While the goods would arrive long after the family, the family would have them in Shanghai—eventually.

THE NAZIS INTERFERE

One problem with requesting permission to leave Germany was that it brought the requester to the attention of the Nazi authorities. More than a few people were collected up and sent to concentration camps after reporting to the travel offices to request exit visas.

Shortly after Kurt's trip to Hamburg to obtain tickets, he was ordered to report to a Nazi office complex. He dutifully did as he was told but did not return. After a few hours of fretting, Lilly's mother decided that she would have to take things into her hands or her family might be ruined. She presented herself at the office where Kurt had reported and informed them that either he could be released to support his family or the Nazi Party could support the family for him. This was a brazen move, even for a member of the National Socialist Party.

Highly decorated Wehrmacht officers,[i] who had relationships with women who were as little as one-eighth Jewish descent, hid either the relationship or the ancestry of the lady in question from the authorities, so a civilian marching into Nazi offices and demanding that a 100 percent Jewish man be released was brave or foolhardy. The truth is that it was desperation. Except for travel approval, things were set for them to leave, and now Kurt might not be able to go. No doubt she had little interest in uprooting her family and taking them to a completely foreign environment without him.

The officials at the first office sent her to another. Since she was alone and we do not have record of what transpired, it is interesting to imagine what might have happened there. It is known that the officials told her not to be foolish, to divorce her Jewish husband, and to move on with her life. But the net result was that Kurt was allowed to come home to get his affairs in order. A return to those offices would be the last the family would ever see of him, so time became a critical factor. Still they had no permission to leave Germany.

PREPARATIONS BY NIGHT

The packing flew into a frenzy at this point. In a cast, Lilly could not help with much, but she was given scissors and newspaper to cut into strips to make packing material while everyone else packed what was left in the house. There were several days before arrangements could be made to leave, and during this time, they took great pains to make certain that no one was aware of their preparations. The children were to mention nothing to their friends; parents did not let neighbors into the apartment, and they essentially isolated themselves from the very German society that had been their home for their entire lives. Since that society had already isolated them, it was a fitting end to their participation.

The things they were packing now were to be transported in the hold of a cargo ship, and the crew to load it came in the middle of the night. At that time Berlin was under blackout orders, and the slightest hint of light coming from windows would draw attention of the authorities, something to be avoided at all costs. So the crates were moved in the dark of night by men who were little more than shadowy figures and taken to the train station. Because the authorities were walking the streets and looking for signs of blackout violations, the trips into and out of the Isaack apartment had to be timed so that those walking beats did not see packers moving things in the middle of the night. It is worthwhile pondering if these movers were more motivated to defy the authorities in this way by profits or humanity. No doubt there was a mix of both.

One thing Lilly thinks as an adult is that Mrs. Isaack must have shipped those goods under her maiden name, or a red flag would truly have been raised in Nazi headquarters. But she was too young for such details to have been shared with her at the time.

It is hard to imagine the difficulty presented by all of this when you read about it in a modern living room, surrounded by neighbors who are not hostile, with comfortable jobs, and in relationships that are constant or at least that do not leave one in constant fear of the secret police. And yet they rose to the occasion. Taking secret trips to distant cities, getting berths on a ship to unknown ports, shipping everything the family owned on a strange liner to meet up at the final destination, not telling neighbors, even hiding any hint from the neighbors while telling their young children that it could mean all their lives if they told their friends, and trusting people you did not know to take your worldly possessions away and deliver them months later to you in another part of the world. Worrying about anyone who appeared to show too much interest in what was going on in your life.

The story of the rise of the Nazi Party and its very heavy impact upon the lives of Jewish citizenry (among others) should serve as a warning against the type of state-sponsored bigotry that the Nazis have come to represent in modern times, but it should also serve as an example of how far people can reach and what they are capable of when oppression rears its ugly head. Not only the Isaack family and their near-miraculous escape from Nazi Germany but also the friend in Hamburg who got them tickets out of Europe, the family in Switzerland who helped with money, the movers who knew that their own livelihoods would be in jeopardy if they were caught transporting goods for Jews, all these people and many more rose above the requirements of daily life to quietly combat oppression.

But now that their household was gone to a freight line, they needed to get to the passenger line. Their connections severed, tickets in hand, the Isaacks, including Lilly and her cast, had to find a way over the Alps to Italy. On July 22, 1939, the family gathered one last time to say their good-byes. Lilly's grandmother gave both girls silver Star of David necklaces and told them to wear them when they were in a place where it would be safe to do so. She told them when they wore them to think of her.

The next day, the Isaacks going to Shanghai—Lilly, her brother and sister, her parents, and her uncle and aunt—left Germany, they assumed, forever.

Chapter 2

FLEEING GERMANY

This is why I weep and my eyes overflow with tears. No one is near to comfort me, no one to restore my spirit. My children are destitute because the enemy has prevailed.

—LAMENTATIONS 1:16

By July 22, Lilly's cast covered both sides of her body, from the armpits to toes. There was no chance of her walking anywhere, and the family had to get from Berlin to Naples, part of the trip on foot.

TO ITALY

This was a heart-wrenching experience for the entire family, and yet the ability to think clearly and find practical solutions to difficult problems was still present. Sometimes necessity truly is the mother of invention. In order to transport Lilly, her mother had acquired a stroller (pram) and modified it to support the weight of a seven-year-old girl plus a plaster cast that covered most of her body. This allowed the family to pass itself off as out with a sick child or with a disabled child, and the ploy was successful enough, as far as it went. In fact, Lilly remembers people avoiding looking at her when they were out with the pram.

There was no safe way that a family lacking papers could travel via train out of Berlin, so they traveled during the night and laid low during the day, getting as far from Berlin as possible, as quickly as possible. The goal was the base of a pass through the mountains where Germany, Italy, and France met and where a train that *was* safe to ride would take them away from Germany and the threat that it now represented.

In order to protect their identities in case they were stopped for a search, Mrs. Isaack put the girls' Star of David necklaces into a deep pocket on the pram and pushed them way down into the pocket, counting on the fact that it would require a pretty-thorough search to find those necklaces.

They were able to get to the train and onto it with the help of a conductor who showed very little interest in examining their papers. He lacked interest so much that Lilly is uncertain to this day if he was sympathetic to the flight of a family with three children fleeing Germany or had been well paid not to be too curious about who this family was. They rode a train up into the St. Bernard Pass and had to switch trains to make the descending journey down into Italy. While transferring from the upbound train to the downbound one, the pram was left behind, as the children were rushed to their berth to get out of sight as soon as possible.

When the girls discovered they were leaving and that the pram was still on the train platform, their composure finally broke down. The pressure of not telling anyone they were going, the stress of their parents seeming to watch every person and every step, and the constant admonitions not to draw attention, all became wrapped up in the necklaces from their grandmother, still pushed down deep into the pocket on the pram. They did not want to leave those necklaces, and they began to wail and cry about it.

The pressure this must have created among adults who were doing all that they could to be unobtrusive and quietly sneak out of the country is difficult to imagine. There was little that could be done to calm Lilly, and she cried most of the way to Rome.

Not only that, but without the pram, her father or uncle would have to carry her whenever walking was required. This made staying unobtrusive rather difficult, but they endeavored to make the remainder of the trip in this manner.

But perhaps the most unsettling part of leaving the pram at the station with two Star of David necklaces in it was that the German authorities would eventually find out about it, and it would be a short jump to realizing that there was a Jewish family on the run. Now they had to worry about being actively followed. Italy was definitely less hostile to Jews, but Italy was Nazi Germany's closest ally, both geographically and politically. The Italians would not hesitate to help find fugitives if the German authorities asked.

TO THE SHIP

Finally, they arrived in Rome. They were not yet free, but a weight was lifting from their shoulders. They still had to take precautions not to get caught, and those precautions were made all the more difficult by the fact that one of the men would have to carry Lilly everywhere they went. It is worth remembering that they did not have visas to be in Italy or anywhere outside of Germany, so the attention carrying a child in a cast would attract was more than they could afford. And thus they took extra steps to be cautious.

Unable to stay in places that would draw attention, they took a room in a run-down hotel for far too much money. As mentioned before, Mrs. Isaack was a fastidious woman, and she bade the children to touch nothing while she inspected the facilities being offered. After a rather-lengthy inspection, she pronounced the accommodations unsuitable for any human to live in. But stay they did because there really was nowhere else to go. It is Lilly's belief that this is the first point at which Mrs. Isaack realized that the life she had known was gone. No doubt the excess amount that was charged for the room was to keep the innkeeper from telling the authorities about them. While it is a terrible thing to think of your fellow people that they would take advantage of those running for their very lives, many would not help refugees for any price, which makes those who profiteered seem a bit more human.

It is a useful exercise to look about at all that life accumulates, the habits that have become part of life, and the things one takes for granted and to consider walking away from it all in a quest for simple survival. This is the world many European Jewish families faced, and those who could not bring themselves to face it, paid a terrible price for their familiarity.

The family stayed in Rome for several days and took the opportunity to see some of the sights. Mr. and Mrs. Isaack were always happy to teach the children about the world, and Naples was new, with history expressed in architecture. They visited St. Peter's Basilica along with many of the churches. Churches in Italy were a relatively safe place to visit, and Rome has many famous ones.

Lilly was still on a strict vegetarian diet and had been so for many months. While in front of the basilica, Mr. Isaack did what the other tourists did; he bought the children hot dogs. Italian hot dogs are made from sausage and include spices with the meat. After months of vegetarian food, Lilly's stomach revolted from the sudden influx of spicy meat, and there in front of the basilica, she began to get violently ill. While trying not to draw attention to yourself, this is not exactly the scenario you want to enact. People looked on but seemed to feel that her father had the child well in hand. Considering that she was in a body cast, was physically ill, and didn't speak Italian, it was lucky that people passed on and let them be.

Anyone who has raised children can probably relate to the fact that trips to safe places like churches were more than likely as much to occupy three children whose world had completely changed and to wear them out enough to sleep at night as to offer lessons in culture and architecture.

After a few days, it was time for their last leg of travel on the European continent. They packed up what they had with them and traveled from Rome to Naples to meet the *Terukuni Maru*, destination Shanghai.

THE *TERUKUNI MARU*

M. S. TERUKUNI MARU 11,600 TONS.
日本郵船株式會社モーターシツプ照國丸總噸壹千六百噸

To a girl from a landlocked city, the *Terukuni Maru* was big and beautiful. One of the better ocean liners of her time, she had come into operation in September 1930 and sailed the southern route from Japan to Europe and back, her normal route going from Nagoya to Osaka to Kobe to Moji and then across to Shanghai, Hong Kong, Singapore, Penang, and Colombo before entering the Suez Canal and calling at Beirut, Naples, Marseilles, and Casablanca and then across to London and back.

To a small child, it must have seemed a wonderland. The ship was over five hundred feet long and sixty-four feet wide, and Lilly was in awe as she was being carried up the gangplank. There was room for 249 passengers (of all classes) on the ship and a crew of 177. Their berths were good, and they were soon ensconced in their rooms. The ship was decked out in luxury, almost to the point of decadence, and to a seven-year-old, it was glamorous.

Lilly still had dietary restrictions. She still needed to eat a primarily vegetarian diet, as was the best medical thought of the day for cases of polio, but the crew was happy to take care of those requirements for her. Her cast quickly became a bigger problem. The family definitely had a sense of humor, and children will be children, no matter how much the world is changing around them. The problem with her cast was not the cast in and of itself but rather children having fun. Her brother Joe decided to have some fun by telling her stories involving people in large casts sinking to the bottom of the ocean and drowning from their casts. Pointing out that ships sank all the time, he told her that if the ship was hit by lightning, it would sink, and she would drown.

His storytelling had more of an impact on young Lilly perhaps than he'd planned. She was so upset that she could not be consoled short of removing the cast. It is likely her parents actually did care about what would happen should the ship go down, but it is also likely that they were aware that she would need the cast off when they reached Shanghai and that there would be a recovery period after it was removed. Of course, along with the removal of Lilly's cast, her brother also had a layer of skin removed from his posterior for creating the emergency while they were still trying to lay low. So it was that the cast was removed shortly before the ship left Naples, and Lilly started to relearn how to walk. Not that one forgets how to walk, but the muscles had atrophied while they had lain unused in the cast. Unsurprisingly Lilly found that she tired easily walking about the ship, rebuilding those muscles.

In keeping with the family's natural love of learning, geography and history lessons were taught from the deck of the *Terukuni Maru*. It was there that the Isaack children learned of Pompeii and Herculaneum, as the ship sailed past Mount Vesuvius. At night, they saw the lava flow coming off the top of the mountain. The education would continue throughout the trip to Shanghai, and it would just be the beginning of learning about foreign things—for the children would live outside of Germany for the rest of their lives.

Due to their circumstances and the nature of travel to many different ports on the way to Shanghai, the children were given strict instructions not to go with strangers and instead to stay where they could be found at all times—particularly while in port. At the port of Colombo, Ceylon (now Sri Lanka), Lilly became exhausted walking about the ship. She asked permission to go to the cabin and lie down, and Mrs. Isaack told her she could but to remember to lock the cabin door. Lilly did as she was told, lay down, and fell asleep.

At the time, European children were frequently being kidnapped in Colombo. The family went to find Lilly and could not. The door to the cabin was locked, but she did not respond to pounding on the door. The family began to assume the worst. Soon crew members were in the adjoining cabins, pounding on the walls, and still there was no response from inside the cabin. As the captain considered turning the entire ship around to head back to port to report Lilly missing, the crew finally decided to send men down on ropes from the deck above to look into the portholes. There, blissfully sleeping in her bed, was Lilly. She had not just locked the door but had also applied the security lock because her mother had told her to lock the door—and the security lock meant that the berth key would not open the door.

All's well that ends well. Eventually the Isaacks were reunited with their youngest daughter, and the ship did not have to turn about and make an unscheduled delay.

While this was not the last of the excitement on the trip to Shanghai, it was the last that stands out as a memorable experience on the month-long trip.

There are vagaries in every significant sequence of events in the world. It is another stark reminder of how close even a highly motivated family comes to not being able to do what is required to survive. On the return trip from Japan to the United Kingdom, the *Terukuni Maru* had hit a German magnetic mine on its approach to Dover and sank. Had the Isaack family waited even the two-month turnaround time for the ship to return to Naples instead of taking the trip they were booked upon, they would never have left Naples. How many families were stranded by such strange circumstances will likely never be known.

But for the Isaacks, they had got free of the Third Reich, and their adventure was just beginning.

Chapter 3

CITY OF MYSTERY, PARIS OF THE EAST

Most of the refugees fleeing to Shanghai knew very little about the city itself.[ii] They knew that things kept getting worse in Europe and that Shanghai was the only place that allowed people in without extensive paper work and a long wait. Some could only stay out of concentration camps if they agreed to leave Germany within a month. Since a long wait might well mean imprisonment or increasingly rumored death, most believed that it could not be worse in Shanghai than in Europe. Because of the problems they were running from, most chose to take the "Paris of the East" nickname at face value. In truth, the French quarter was originally known as Paris of the East, and only over time did the name come to mean Shanghai more generally. And the city more generally did not deserve the title.

FIRST IMPRESSIONS

As the liners brought the refugees to Shanghai, the reality of their situation no doubt became very clear. There were skyscrapers, a massive port, and European sections of the city that looked the part. But there were also entire sections of the city (most notable upon approach was the Hongkew sector) that had been completely destroyed in the 1937 Sino-Japanese War[iii] and other sections where low, tenement-style houses held the poorer portions of the Chinese population in massively overcrowded conditions. While looking over the city, visitors found that the humidity was oppressive—for those coming in summer, oppressive and hot; for those coming in winter, oppressive and cold—and the humidity held the stench of a city without plumbing close.

The 1937 Sino-Japanese War had been a short, violent fight between the Kuomintang (Chinese Nationalist) Army and the invading Japanese. While the war raged across China specifically and Asia more generally, our interest in the war is with Shanghai. In the end of 1937, Japan defeated the Chinese Nationalist forces in Shanghai and took over all the Chinese-run portions of the city. Since Japan was not at war with other international powers, the International Settlement and the French Concession were left under the control of their respective governments at the time.

On debarking from the cruise liner, the family found that everyone around them was speaking a foreign language, and the foreignness of their new home became reality. As Ursula Bacon, author of *Shanghai Diary*, is quoted in the *Denver Post*, "Boiling under the hot sun and steamed by the humidity in the air was the combination of rotting fruit peelings, spoiled leftovers, raw bones, dead cats, drowned puppies, carcasses of rats, and the lifeless body of a newborn baby, all fermented with human feces and sprinkled with urine from chamber pots, plus clots of blood and lumps."[iv]

The cities of Europe in the 1930s were clean and well kept, not terribly racially diverse, and well ordered across the board. According to analysis done in David Kranzler's excellent book *Japanese, Nazis, and Jews*, the majority of Jewish immigrants were from middle-class families, mostly from those clean European cities.[v]

Shanghai was completely different. For one, Shanghai was one of the world's largest cities, with a population approaching four million people, pretty close to the population of Berlin. Add to this the fact that most of Shanghai did not have running water, that opiate use was rampant, and that poverty was more so. While there were cars in the city, most transport was handled by coolies who pulled or pedaled rickshaws through the streets or who pulled carts to move goods, while merchants carried live poultry on poles over their shoulders to the market, where the birds were slaughtered.

Hongkew district after refugee rebuilding. Photo credit: Yad Vashem Digital Archives

A TINY BIT OF POLITICS

If only those were the worst of Shanghai's problems, though. Due to a strange set of circumstances, Shanghai had no official government. Sections of the city were governed and policed, but in some cases, a criminal had but to cross a street to avoid the police because jurisdictions were that split and the police did not appreciate officers from another section crossing into their jurisdiction. This made putting a stop to any kind of crime nearly impossible.

In addition to policing being divided across the different jurisdictions, most of the police departments suffered from corruption.[vi]

Due to treaties negotiated after China lost the first Opium War with Britain and ensuing treaties negotiated by other nations, parts of Shanghai were extraterritorial, meaning that Chinese law only somewhat applied to citizens of those countries. These sections of the city were independent from the central Shanghai government. They were the French Concession, which was managed, policed, and planned by the French consul general via a committee.

The International Settlement served the same purpose for the other great powers—Belgium, Brazil, Denmark, Italy, Japan, the Netherlands, Norway, Portugal, Spain, Sweden, Switzerland, the United Kingdom, and the United States—via an elected committee called the Shanghai Municipal Council that shared representation although it was mostly dominated by UK, Japanese, and American representatives. In fact, the chairman of the Shanghai Municipal Council was American or British for the entirety of its existence from 1853 until 1942, the last election before Japanese takeover of the International Settlement. That election saw Japan take the chairmanship after decades of Anglo-American leadership.[vii]

The vast majority of the city's population was Chinese, and the majority of those citizens were recent immigrants from outlying districts who had come to Shanghai to avoid fighting between Chinese factions and between the Chinese Nationalist Army and Japan. Due to the sudden influx, housing was in short supply, sanitation was poor, overcrowding was a problem, and death on the streets was commonplace. It cost money to be buried. As many didn't have the money, a loved one in his or her final throes of death would be placed on the street to die, or more often, a dearly departed loved one would be quietly set out on the street the night after he or she passed so that the burden of burying the person was not born by the sometimes-starving family.

Also placed on the street to die were children, when the family could not afford to feed them. It was an accepted, if not encouraged, practice for families to abandon girl children if they were the first child. This problem has existed to one extent or another throughout Chinese history, and it still occurs to some extent today (although relatively recent changes to Chinese government policies have reduced the problem). Some European immigrants learned the hard way that those children were considered unowned and that any who stopped to touch them—or to feed them—became responsible by custom (and, in areas of Chinese control, law) for the maintenance of the child.

Alongside the dead and dying, beggars plied their craft, banging their heads on the sidewalk, or child beggars, chasing after likely prospects, begged for food or change. As with most massed beggars in most cities, to offer something to one beggar was to develop a following of others begging even louder and more insistently.

DISEASE

Disease in Shanghai was rampant. While the native Chinese population and the Europeans who had lived in Shanghai for a long time before 1938 had developed resistance to the more exotic diseases, the new European émigrés did not yet have that same resistance, and enough natives suffered from things like diphtheria and amoebic dysentery that these diseases spread quickly to the new population. While there were doctors available, both in the long-time Shanghai residents (Chinese and European) and in the refugees, medicine was in short supply, something that Lilly and her family would soon discover, as would many other refugees.

Since Shanghai had very little plumbing, there were several ways that waste was disposed of. The one that immigrants would be first exposed to was that people relieved themselves wherever they were when the need arose. Children's clothing was designed such that this could be performed in a busy street without exposing oneself. This, no doubt, shocked newcomers as they made their way to temporary homes and prepared them for the next waste-disposal habit they would encounter. Many households emptied their buckets into the street, not wanting to contaminate their homes with the waste.

The third method of disposal was collection of these buckets in boxed carts so that the waste could be used as fertilizer. Each morning in many neighborhoods, a man would come through with a cart for waste, and families would empty their buckets into the cart—often the cart man paid a small fee, sometimes not. The cartful of "honey," as it was called, would then be sold to farmers as fertilizer for crops. Needless to say, fertilizing crops with human waste also contributed to the disease problem. If fruits and vegetables were not thoroughly washed, diseases carried by any contributors to the "honey pot" could be—and often were—passed on.

And there were yet more challenges the refugees had to face. Housing was dear, not just because a large number of Chinese had come to escape fighting in the countryside. The Sino-Japanese War of 1937, barely a year before the first refugees arrived, had left large swaths of the city in ruins. There had been no time or materials to rebuild most of this damage.

This was both a blessing and a curse because the ruined portions of the city—particularly the Hongkew sector, right next to the International Settlement—were the most affordable bits of land to be had. Many refugees had been stripped of funds on their way out of Germany and, along with those with no contacts in other countries to send them money, had little choice but to settle in the ruins. Even with the help of the established Jewish communities, there were not many other opportunities to set out on their own.

Consequently, those who could bought ruins or abandoned warehouse space and transformed them into places to live—but that is getting ahead of the story. For now, it is enough to know that refugees faced a daunting future in Shanghai, due not only to problems in hygiene, crime, and overcrowding but also to strangeness of the environment.

THERE WERE BRIGHT SPOTS

While conditions in Shanghai were far from perfect for the refugees, there were some bright spots that showed nearly immediately upon arrival.

There was help available. Two established Jewish communities made it a point to help the refugees as they arrived. One community was primarily from Russia, and they were known as the Ashkenazi Jews. The other community was from the Middle East, and they were known as the Sephardim or Baghdadi Jews. These two groups could not be more different. The Ashkenazi were largely stateless or only tenuously retaining their Russian (and sometimes Polish) citizenship, were mostly in the lower classes (though having a better life than most Chinese), and were the larger of the two groups, at around five thousand members. The Baghdadi Jews were a small contingent of roughly seven hundred people, mostly wealthy British Commonwealth citizens. Several of them were knighted, and they largely controlled business and trade in the Shanghai community. But both groups cared for their less-fortunate brethren who had been forced to leave everything behind and come to Shanghai.

The men's section of one of the *heime* maintained for refugees.
Photo credit: Yad Vashim Digital Archives

They had committees common to Jewish communities across the globe that handled civil and religious issues and directed charity. In the case of the Shanghai committees, most notable were the International Committee for European Immigrants (IC) and the Committee for the Assistance of European Jewish Refugees in Shanghai (CFA). Among the many services these organizations offered, they requested financial assistance from around the globe. There were several points in the decade from 1938 to 1948 where assistance from Jewish committees around the globe saved lives of many of the poorer immigrants.

The committees quickly built *heime* (homes) to temporarily house new arrivals and house the indigent for longer stretches of time. While there were plans for custom buildings designed for the influx, money was tight and the influx large, so existing warehouses, factories, or hospitals that had been abandoned were purchased and fitted out as group housing. The *heime* were a blessing and a curse, allowing the poorest refugees the ability to sleep somewhere other than in the streets and offering a place for new arrivals to stay while they made living arrangements. But they were crowded. Very, very crowded, with bunks sometimes as many as six stacked and several families in a single small room.

The Japanese had taken over the Chinese portions of the city after the 1937 Sino-Japanese War, and the Japanese, too, were well disposed toward the immigrants. They had learned anti-Semitism from White Russians, who had helped translate the *Protocols of the Elders of Zion* in the early twentieth century; the Japanese believed in the worldwide Jewish conspiracy described in the book, and their own history told them it was probably true.[viii] At the turn of the century, a Jewish banker from New York had taken a chance and loaned them money to finance a war with Russia. Once they had been given a chance by one banker, other bankers also loaned them money, and eventually with their new armaments purchased via those loans, the Japanese had won the war.

As Japan grew closer to Nazi Germany, this view of Jewish-controlled banking and governments as a global cabaal grew more entrenched. But Japan had no history with anti-Semitism, and the filters that Europe used to discriminate against Jewish people did not exist. As such, the Japanese came to the logical conclusion that the Jewish citizens of Shanghai, coming from many countries, could be of assistance through this supposed shadowy international power organization in their quest to unite Asia. Acting on the belief that there *was* a worldwide Jewish cabal and that treating Jewish citizens in Asia well might convince this cabal to help them, the Japanese government made it a point of policy to treat the Jewish communities across China and Japan fairly.

This, too, saved many lives as Germany began to pressure Japan to exterminate its Jewish population toward the end of the war, but the differences between Japan and Germany also showed upon arrival by the Japanese giving the Jewish committees free reign to help refugees. Even though the Japanese were very firm in their public pronouncements about supporting the Jewish people, they were close to Germany prior to the Tripartite Pact, which established working relationships and exchange of technical (military) information. After the signing of the pact in 1940, Japan was effectively a Nazi ally, and this friendship hung like a shroud over refugees.

With access to the records of and the leisure to examine Japanese internal communications, we know now that the Jewish community in Shanghai was never in danger of death camps, and yet the SS representative in Shanghai had drawn up a plan for the Japanese that did include death camps. While the Japanese flatly rejected this plan, the mere presence of SS officers in Shanghai must have driven fear into the refugees, whether they knew of such plans or not, increasing the stress introduced in their new environment.

And this hot, smelly, raucous, overcrowded, multinational city largely under the control of a country friendly to those who wanted to imprison and kill all Jewish peoples was suddenly and definitively going to be home. From the view of the refugees, it might just be their home permanently.

Chapter 4

SETTLING INTO SHANGHAI

Asia was much warmer than Germany, but while the *Terekuni Maru* was on the open ocean and moving, there was a breeze that kept the discomfort to a minimum. As the ship sailed up the Whangpoo River toward Shanghai's International Settlement, the ship was moving slower, the open ocean breeze was gone, and the sights, smells, and sounds of the city penetrated to the deck of the ship. For weeks, the Isaack family and many others had traveled on a luxury liner with all that such transport had to offer: fine meals, swimming pools, private rooms, fresh air.

A NEW HOME?

They wondered what their life in this new place would be like, of course. The ship sailed past other ships of several nations, including warships of both the United Kingdom and the Empire of Japan, and slid up to the dock. The passengers gathered their things—in the case of the Isaacks, that was very little, as most of their possessions had been freight shipped and they had traveled light when fleeing Germany—and filed off the ship. It was August 26, 1939, and already Shanghai was a closing port. Those not already at sea would require visas to enter Shanghai, effectively meaning that Shanghai too was closed to refugees from Europe.

On the gangplank, as the family looked across the crowded wharf, the oppressive smells of the city and the chatter of too many people talking at once in a foreign language wafted over them. Mrs. Isaack said to her husband, "Kurt, what have we gotten ourselves into?"

It was a valid question and one she no doubt thought many more times over the next nine years.

TO THE *HEIM*

As mentioned earlier, the Jewish communities of Shanghai were organized and made every effort to see that refugees were properly oriented in Shanghai so that they could begin their new lives. The first sign the refugees saw of this organization was trucks waiting for them at the pier. These refugees, some wearing their best clothes from their former lives, walked up planks to stand or sit in the back of transport trucks and were driven through the city.

Along the way, the Isaacks and the other refugees were given their first glimpse of Shanghai. Dirty streets, beggars, multitudes of people, and hand transport was the norm for most things—from people to goods to livestock. But the Isaack family didn't see most of Shanghai. They were transported through the International Settlement, one of the cleanest sections of Shanghai with architecture that was familiar to anyone from Europe, and into the Hongkew district. The Hongkew district was one of the worst districts in the city. Officially claimed by the Japanese, the residents were mostly Chinese and mostly poor, with a few Japanese living among them. Hongkew had been largely destroyed in an artillery duel and continued fighting during the 1937 Sino-Japanese War. While the residents had begun rebuilding, not much of an effort had been made yet, and people lived in ruins or abandoned buildings.

The truck took them to one of the *heime*, and they were given a meal and cots to sleep in. While the arrangements gave them a roof over their heads and two meals a day, it was not anything at all like they were accustomed to.

One of Lilly's more vibrant memories from her times in the *heime* is of the restrooms, a board across a large room, partitions separating holes in the board that were only about four inches across. Users lined themselves up with the hole and relieved themselves in this relatively public setting. The refuse dropped into holes in the floor that Lilly assumes had buckets that could be removed and emptied. Her assumption is based on the fact that some facilities were used throughout their time in Shanghai, yet the floors were cement. Her memory is vivid because of the bugs, though. Large bloodsucking beetles would wait for someone to sit on the board and then bite from below. While the type of insect was not known, anything that bit and drew blood could spread disease, and this no doubt contributed to the Shanghailanders' woes.

Mr. Isaack set out to improve their housing situation nearly immediately. The problem was that Shanghai had a housing shortage. Seventeen thousand refugees were emigrating from Europe in the course of just a little over a year whereas a year before the Isaacks had arrived, large swaths of the city had been reduced to rubble. After four days, he had secured a place for them to live. As they didn't have much in the way of possessions, moving was not a problem. They left the *heime* and moved into their small, new home.

CONTINUED POLIO TREATMENTS

Lilly was checked into the hospital nearly immediately upon arrival in Shanghai. She was too young to know for certain why they returned her to the hospital, but she stayed there for a short time and was back with her family by December 1939. While she was in the hospital, the doctors tried to use traction to treat the residual effects of her polio but to no avail. They determined that her limp was caused by actual physical damage and that she would need to learn how to live with her situation. While at the hospital, Lilly met Erika, a friendship that would last the rest of their lives. At one point while the two of them were in the hospital, hospital staff discovered that the girls were missing from their ward. After a search, they were discovered...in the surgery prep room, washing their hair in the sinks where doctors normally scrubbed. It was not the last trouble the two would find themselves in during their lives in Shanghai.

THE SJYA AND THE KADOORIE SCHOOL

Upon release from the hospital, Lilly was promptly enrolled in the Kadoorie School, more properly known as the Shanghai Jewish Youth Association (SJYA) School. The school was a testament to the types of things that the existing Jewish community did for the refugees. Horace Kadoorie had seen a need for refugee children to be schooled. The school at the International Settlement and the single private Jewish school could not possibly accommodate the influx of refugee children, and yet the children would need an education. So he organized funds and founded the SJYA School. The funds for the school came almost exclusively from Jewish people and groups who had been in Shanghai for a longer period of time. Sir Kadoorie, with help from others in the Shanghai Jewish community, saw to it that the children had qualified teachers and, when times became difficult, a meal each day for years. For some children, that meal would be a lifesaver when they were in need.

Since arriving in Shanghai, Lilly had picked up some Chinese and had applied herself to mastering the language. But upon her arrival at the SJYA School, she discovered that instruction would be mostly in English (although foreign languages, including Japanese and Chinese, were taught). She did not speak much English, and that combined with her time in the hospital led the school to decide to place her a grade behind what her age warranted. Of all the things that Lilly was going through, this was something that she could change. She threw herself into mastering English, practicing as much as possible, and her persistence quickly paid off. In two short weeks, the school reevaluated their decision, and she was moved to the correct grade for her age. School was a lot of fun; for Lilly, it was exhilarating. The school had a varied curriculum. She delved into languages, reading and math, and, that key for all schoolchildren, making friends. And she excelled in her studies. To Lilly's joy, her class included her sister, Ingrid, and her new friend, Erika.

While school was enjoyable for Lilly, there was one teacher with whom Lilly had an antagonistic relationship. Ms. Rosa Lesser asked her on the first day of class, "Do you know Kurt Isaack?" When Lilly replied yes, Ms. Lesser asked, "How?"

Lilly replied, "He's my father."

The conversation ended when Ms. Lesser said, "Oh, God, not another one."

Thereafter if something mischievous occurred or even something simply went wrong, Ms. Lesser, who had taught Mr. Isaack as a child in Germany, assumed that Lilly was the source of the problem. Even though Ms. Lesser had this prejudice, Lilly still says today that this woman was the person who taught her to love mathematics.

SJYA or Kadoorie School, second location

It is worth noting the quality of schooling that the Kadoorie School represented in this time of troubles. While Mr. Kadoorie did not personally finance all of it, he did lead the way and use his financial contributions to create the school, and he also used his influence to find a new location when their original one became unavailable. The school boasted seventeen teachers, taught primarily the Queen's English, and was prepared to teach up to six hundred students.[ix] School was not what most Westerners would consider a standard classroom today. First, the only language spoken on school grounds outside of language classes was English, not the native tongue of the vast majority of students. Second, classes had but one book. The teacher had the book, and the students paid attention throughout class or failed. There were writing materials but most of the time not enough for six hundred students to take notes in every class, so paying attention was the only way to pass. Finally, the classrooms used benches, not desks, with up to four children per bench. Lilly's bench held herself, her sister, and Erika for years of schooling.

THE FATE OF THEIR HOUSEHOLD GOODS

Meanwhile the family had been getting by without the household goods they had shipped to Shanghai. They had waited for months after their arrival in Shanghai and were settling in to life in their new home. But the goods they had shipped would give them things they sorely needed to make a household, and some of the goods might be sold to make much-needed money to help support the family.

The Isaacks were not the only ones to find that the sale of their goods might be useful. While stopped in a port on the way to Shanghai, the cargo ship carrying their household goods along with other cargo needed to pay a massive tariff in Africa, or the ship would be sold at auction to cover the tariff. Having only one ready source of cash, the captain did what was necessary to save his ship: he sold every bit of cargo on it and paid the tariff. Mr. Isaack had always had a sense of humor, and even this disaster was a source of levity to lift family spirits as he described how some monkey really looked cute in Mrs. Isaack's Sunday hat while swinging from tree to tree in Africa. Mr. Isaack's sense of humor would continue to help them survive as things continued to get more difficult.

HOME LIFE

The house they moved into had a small, central courtyard on the ground floor, and cooking was done with a charcoal fueled hibachi. Mrs. Isaack had never cooked on a hibachi, but she took to it as best she could. When cooking was problematic and the family's standard of eating was not anywhere near what they were accustomed to from Europe, the decision was made to spend some of their small amount of funds on a hand-pumped kerosene stove that offered a cooking surface and an even heat. Cooking improved immensely.

Another thing that stoves were used for was to boil water for washing clothes. The Yangtze water would slowly stain clothes and often make those who drank the water ill, so water was never used without boiling. One day, Mrs. Isaack was cooking dinner with a bucket of hot water holding clothes nearby, the stove was overpumped, and fire broke out. Mrs. Isaack, not knowing what to do to control the fire—which could consume the entire house—dumped the bucket of clothes and water on the stove, putting out the fire but scorching some of the clothes. Quick thinking saved the day, but clothes they could ill afford to lose were ruined. Another showing of Mr. Isaack's sense of humor is that he walked in, looked at the wash water over the dinner, clothes, and all, and blandly asked, "So what's for dinner?" Mrs. Isaack chased him out with the mop.

Speaking of laundry, this first house that the Isaacks lived in was in a town-house-style arrangement, and next door was a Chinese laundry. The children found a hole in the wall between the laundry and their rooms, and at night they would watch the laundry in operation. The pressing part of the operation left them with an impression for the rest of their lives. The press operation consisted of a man who would suck water into his mouth from a shallow bowl, spray it out upon the clothes, and then press them with an iron. With all the squalor that Shanghai offered, this was one of the largest impressions that Lilly took away. For the rest of her life, she did not use laundry services if she could avoid it.

It is an interesting observation that adjustment must have been harder for the adults than the children. The children believed that as long as their parents were there, all would be well. But the adults looked at war damage, rats the size of rabbits, refuse in the streets, and even bodies and wondered what they had stepped into, while the children knew that while they were holding their parents' hands, all was basically OK with the world. As an adult, Lilly wonders about what must have gone through her parents' minds in those first few months.

DEALING WITH DISEASE

As discussed in chapter 3, illness was rampant the entire time that the refugees stayed in Shanghai, but the first few months and then later, in the first few months after the Japanese established the ghetto, were the worst. Shortly after arriving in Shanghai, both Mr. and Mrs. Isaack suffered from exotic diseases that they had not been exposed to in Europe. Mr. Isaack contracted typhoid, and while treatment kept him alive, the disease did serious long-term damage. In a short time, he dropped from 220 to 120 pounds. Mrs. Isaack contracted meningitis, thankfully at a different time, and she was also in the hospital. At this time, the children were constantly sick, but nothing so bad as to need hospitalization. Yet.

After Mr. Isaack's close call—he now stood six feet four inches and weighed only 120 pounds—Mrs. Isaack took to cleansing all the food the family consumed. The feces-as-fertilizer process that China had used successfully for centuries did not hold up well in a port city with people passing through from all around the world, not to mention the crowding and sanitary challenges in Shanghai. This is no surprise. Much of the rampant disease that swept through Shanghai was borne in agricultural products. Because of this threat, Mrs. Isaack began either cooking all produce very thoroughly or washing it in what Lilly calls *übermangal kale*. This purple liquid stained the food it was used to wash, but the magnesium and potassium mixture was a rather-powerful disinfectant. So while the vegetables Lilly ate from this point forward were either overcooked or purple tinged, the family relied upon these processes to help them avoid the sweeping disease in the city.

One day early in 1941, Mr. Isaack came home with a child. To this day, Lilly remembers the look on her mothers' face as she carefully asked, "Kurt, where did you get that baby?" As happened with many refugee families, those who had so little lent a hand to those who had nothing. Mr. Isaack explained that a friend of his had found himself a single father of two with no way to take care of his children and that Mr. Isaack had told his friend that Mrs. Isaack wouldn't mind taking care of one of them since she loved children. Thus, Daisy Israel, whom the family called Pitsi, came to live with the Isaacks for a time and was treated as one of their own children.

It is worth mentioning at this point that the Chinese people accepted the Jewish communities in their city. The established (Ashkenazi and Sephardim) Jewish communities had businesses and shops that were frequented by Chinese citizens of the city, and of course, those shops could not exist without suppliers—many of them Chinese businesses. Though there was plenty of reason for the poorer of the Chinese to be resentful that refugees came and competed with them for work, Lilly remembers nothing of the kind, and they were accepted into the community without much ado as they learned the mores and standards of this foreign land.

In October 1941, Mrs. Isaack went into the hospital to deliver the family's fourth official baby (fifth, if Pitsi is counted). Due to complications, both she and the lovely baby, named Marion Helene Mable Isaack, were kept in the hospital much longer than the normal fourteen-day convalescence of the time. She would come home to a completely different world than the one she'd left for the hospital. The Isaacks' life was changing yet again.

Chapter 5

THE TROUBLE DEEPENS

One would think that after leaving all that they owned, a life of relative comfort, and family for the remote shores of a foreign land, struggling for housing and food, and learning new languages, customs, and mores, fate would be done dealing harshly with the refugees, but it had just begun.

As mentioned previously, the Japanese did have their own version of anti-Semitism, which believed in a worldwide Jewish conspiracy. Part of their beliefs held that the United States was run—through the president and secretary of state—by this worldwide Jewish conspiracy. It was this belief in the conspiracy that led the Japanese to allow several first-class Jewish schools to prosper in portions of Shanghai that they controlled. A segment of Japanese leadership believed that when they won the war, the students in those schools, all multilingual, would be ambassadors to their newly acquired subject-countries. The only request the Japanese authorities had made of the schools was that they teach Japanese. The Japanese authorities in Shanghai even facilitated international Jewish organizations' attempts to send funds to Shanghai so that the refugees could more easily be taken care of.

PEARL HARBOR

There were limits to Japanese largesse. There had been an internal debate about who was their enemy and where the war should be taken. Eventually it was determined that while Russia was the enemy, the United States was the greater threat, since Russia was involved in a war with Germany and America was a force upon the sea.

Once Operation Barbarossa, the German invasion of Russia, had been launched, the Japanese knew that their nearby enemy would be busy. Thus, it was decided to attack the United States, the United Kingdom, and Holland with violent force. On December 7, 1941 (December 8 in Shanghai due to the International Date Line), those countries' possessions were attacked across the Pacific and Asia.

At the same time, Japanese marines—the Special Naval Landing Force—marched into Shanghai's International Settlement and took control of the area from the international tribunal, which had run it until then.

Things immediately became tenser for the refugees, as the ally of the government they had run from had just taken over the one area of Shanghai they did not previously control. (The French concession was Vichy French, allies of Germany and thus an ally of Japan and worked with the Japanese for unified governance of the city.)

The first effect of Japanese attacks against the allies was the internment of all nationals of hostile countries. That included most of the Sephardic Jewish community, who were largely British citizens. The Sephardic Jews had done much to care for the refugees, some of whom had failed to adapt and all of whom found it difficult to obtain and maintain jobs in a tough environment. With the arrest of these worthies and their placement in internment camps, Sephardic assistance was suddenly cut off, and those remaining in the aid associations scrambled to fill the gaps it created.

The next impact was the discovery that the United States, whose Jewish communities had also been providing assistance to the aid societies, had a policy against sending large sums of money into territory occupied by an enemy of war. Suddenly nearly all assistance from America was stopped, as it became treason to send money into land occupied by the Japanese. This put the aid societies and families who had been receiving funds from family in America in a tough financial situation.

Lilly was too young to pay attention to the interaction of nations, but the loss of funds for the aid societies constricted everyone. The poor had less money to spend, and those who were better off spent only what they truly needed to, holding the rest against worse times that they were certain would come. Jobs disappeared, and businesses closed, while the uncertainty of being considered hostile by the occupying forces drew a shadow over everything. The children knew that Mr. Kadoorie, the man their school was named after, had been put into a prison camp on the outskirts of Shanghai. That fact alone must have weighed more heavily on them than the wrangling of nations.

The sudden reduction in cash weighed heavily on a population that was barely making ends meet, and many refugee businesses were forced to close. Those who were barely scraping by, and many of those who lost businesses, suddenly found themselves moving to the most affordable section of the city: the ruins of Hongkew, only somewhat rebuilt after the 1937 Sino-Japanese altercations. If not for the *heime*, many more would have starved in those days. As it were, many people were crammed into small, overcrowded living spaces with available food reduced, as the buying power of the aid associations shrank.

RETURN TO THE *HEIM*

The Isaack family lost their business. They were one of many families who moved into Hongkew. As with other relocations, the Isaack family started their life in Hongkew humbly. Their first home in the ghetto was a large room with sixteen families crammed into it. The bunks were stacked four high, and Lilly remembers that privacy was not a luxury that anyone in that room had. The Isaacks had always been a close family, no doubt part of what helped them persevere. It was in this room that Lilly discovered for the first time that not all families were steeped in love and working together for all things.

The father of one family was a violinist and was teaching his daughter Dita to play accordion. Everyone else living in the room, with little more to do, would perch on the bunks and watch the lessons. Not because there would be beautiful music in the course of the lesson but because the lessons nearly always ended in a family feud, which was treated as a form of entertainment. It was here, largely because of Dita's family, that Lilly learned that not all families were as tightly knit and loving as hers was. It was inconceivable to her that her father would ever consider treating her in the manner that Dita's father treated the girl.

As an adult, Lilly can see that the stress and uncertainties played a large role in these disagreements, bringing out the worst in people, but then, as a child, she learned that her family was special. The truth is that the strength of the family is what has maintained countless people in times of strife or loss; it is just that the severity and length of the trials faced by the refugees almost demanded a strong family, while throughout history, strong families have generally been a boon but not so central to survival. It *is* a testament to the Isaack family that they held together through blow after blow and had the wherewithal to withstand the troubles, but this is a testament to many, if not most, refugee families.

But there was real entertainment in the room also. Many of those who lived with the Isaacks were members of the theater, a career that fell prey to the reduced incomes of the refugee communities. Some were talented opera performers and would put on impromptu shows or simply tell stories to occupy the children's minds in the evenings.

In this overcrowded room, Mr. Isaack showed his steadfast optimism once again by telling the children that the situation the family was in was temporary and that one day they would be able to stick their tongues out at Mr. Hitler. The thought of acting so irreverently to the man they saw as both powerful and responsible for their situation cheered the Isaack children. Lilly remembers this imagery of her father to this very day as a thing that cheered her in the midst of their dire situation.

It was to this room that Mrs. Isaack brought home their new baby. Small and frail, Marion was a source of anxiety for Mr. and Mrs. Isaack. The children noticed what had been happening all along—that their parents would eat less so that there was more for the children. They also noticed that the new baby needed basic nutrition. Thus, they resolved to tell their parents what they had learned, that they were not hungry, in the hopes of Marion getting more food. But even with a little extra food, Marion was a baby and could just cry. As time went on and Marion became able to eat adult food, this became less of a problem, but born into poverty and near famine, subjected to the sweeping illnesses that a tropical climate brings, Marion remained small and frail while growing just the same.

ANOTHER NEW HOME

One day, Mr. Isaack came home to inform the family that he had found them a new home. In the overcrowding of the only partially restored Hongkew, he had found a place that had only one other family in the room. It was a smaller room, but it would only be ten people living in that room—four adults and six children. The family happily moved to the less crowded environment. The joy that they felt at the increased perception of privacy cannot be overstated. While there was still no privacy, perhaps only one or two people would be watching at a time. The room was smaller and on the second floor. But it was home, and they settled in.

Food became a serious problem for all the refugees, and the amount that was available was reduced due to several factors combined. Because of the Sino-Japanese War that had raged through (and was still raging through in some areas) the Chinese countryside, there were less crops available. The initiation of war with the allied nations had reduced imports to near nothing, and that same declaration of war had cut off many sources of aid that largely went to refugees. The Red Cross still operated in Shanghai, but its budget was severely cut by the withdrawal of monies from the allied countries. The JDC was still operational, but again funds had nearly dried up; they were in fact in a worse position than the Red Cross. The Sephardim, who were the people in Shanghai who had managed feeding of the refugees in the most desperate need, were in an internment camp, and thus organizing food for the *heime* was thrown into disarray.

Already the shortage of food was being felt. Hunger started to become a common friend. People either talked of the fine foods or of Europe constantly or tried not to talk of food at all. The Isaacks talked of this being temporary. But the shadow of the Japanese government's alliance with Nazi Germany hung over them, and the hunger continued.

The Japanese government slowly asserted increased control of government of the entire city. Their presence was seen everywhere, and while the Japanese authorities were wise enough to continue to use the Sikh traffic police, who were both efficient and well respected in the community, though they had ties to the British Empire, the adjudication of justice felt the increasing pressure of the Japanese authorities, as did refugee-aid societies. There were several changes in the year after the Japanese takeover of the city, but they were a slowly tightening noose, not the visceral shock of the sudden movements that took place in Germany before the refugees left. Still, restrictions were slowly being leveled on everyone, regardless of nationality, as Japan moved to make the swaths of China they controlled into a part of the Empire of Japan.

ESTABLISHMENT OF THE RESTRICTED AREA

Finally, after more than a year of slowly gathering control about them, on February 8, 1943, the Japanese took the step everyone feared. Swaths of Jewish citizens were forced to relocate into a small restricted area in Shanghai known as the Hongkew district. The influence of the German government was felt in the extreme in this announcement. Only those stateless Jews who had arrived after 1937 had to relocate. This left the vast majority of the Russian (Ashkenazi) Jews outside of the controlled area. Since most of the Ashkenazi were White Russian and against Germany's archenemy, the source of this order was pretty obvious. With few exceptions, German and Eastern European Jews were to be interned while others remained free to come and go as they pleased.

The refugees must truly have wondered, "Is this the beginning of the end?" because word was seeping across the globe about places like the Warsaw Ghetto and even (in the international press) places like Treblinka. Although it was all rumor and innuendo and most people didn't believe the more extreme stories, they still existed, and the stories had to make the Jewish refugees wonder as they moved their things to the designated area under the eyes of soldiers placed there to control the refugees.

For the Isaacks, the eight thousand refugees, and the tens of thousands of Chinese nationals already living in Hongkew, overcrowding suddenly got much worse, as eight thousand more people moved into the nine square miles of the Hongkew ghetto.

Chapter 6

LIFE IN THE GHETTO

Devastation in Hongkew, 1937. Photo courtesy of Fred Isaack

On February 18, 1943, the Japanese authorities declared the Hongkew district a restricted area that all stateless refugees who had arrived after 1937 and had their citizenship revoked by their home country must move into. At this time, there were around one hundred ten thousand people living in Hongkew, and roughly eight thousand refugees would have to move to the ghetto. The total size of the ghetto was less than one square mile, and it was still damaged from the 1937 Sino-Japanese War.

It is worthwhile here to make very clear that the Japanese authorities did not use the term "ghetto." They referred to the "restricted area," and Judaism was not mentioned. But the detailed definition of stateless refugee made it clear the target was the Jewish refugees. This is important because Nazi representatives to the Empire of Japan had put forward a plan that would have created a concentration camp, including medical experiments on prisoners and enforced starvation and everything else that came with European concentration camps. The Japanese compromised with the Germans while protecting their Jewish citizens' lives. No matter the Japanese motivation, those who survived the ensuing years in Shanghai owe their survival, at least to some extent, to the empire.

Things were already tight for those who lived in Shanghai, but the movement of so many more people into Hongkew on top of the issues that already plagued them started the worst phase of life for the refugees in Shanghai.

The Japanese authorities did not assist families moving to the ghetto but merely ordered them to move by May 18, moving both businesses and homes. With so many homes coming on the market at once, the refugees sold their homes for a small fraction of their value and then found that existing housing inside Hongkew was hard to find, even for those with the funds to pay for it.

FOR THE LOVE OF CHILDREN

As happens in families no matter the circumstance, the Isaacks paid much attention to Marion. The baby of the family normally gets attention from adoring older sisters, and a mother whose attention goes to those who need it most. But amid the squalor and problems of Shanghai, a young child was a treasure.

One day, Mrs. Isaack mentioned to Mr. Isaack that they didn't even have a picture of Marion. At two years old, there had been neither money nor opportunity to have a sitting with a photographer, and the Isaacks had lost all their household goods on the trip to China. Lilly and her older sister spent time and effort collecting bits of yarn and rewinding them. The balls of yarn they created by twining all the little bits of yarn they could lay their hands on could be sold to others for making clothes. By this method, the girls were collecting money, secretly going about the task of making certain their mother had a picture of the youngest child in the family.

The Hongkew ghetto was not fenced in: it was simply guarded by Jewish members of the city's auxiliary police, a mandatory civilian-service group known as the Pao Chi organized the year before.[x] While the Pao Chi were sympathetic to the plight of the refugees, when it was their turn to guard, they had to be careful of being too lenient. The Japanese authorities held the Pao Chi responsible, and Japanese soldiers performed spot checks on access points. With that said, some members of the Pao Chi were more enthusiastic about guard duty than others, and it did happen that some turned in those leaving the ghetto or returning to it without a proper pass to the Japanese authorities.

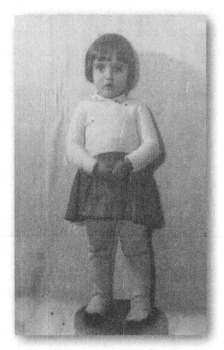

Knowing this, Lilly and Ingrid took Marion and the collection of cast-off bits they had gathered out of the ghetto without a pass one day. If you catch her in a relaxed moment, Lilly will tell you that the children knew ways in and out of the ghetto that were not available to adults. No doubt that is true, as children do always seem to know the hidey-holes and unorthodox exits from a given area. Even as children, this was a dangerous decision, but they hoped to barter for a picture of Marion.

They had lived in Shanghai for years at this point and knew their way around. They found a photographer who took their offer of rewound yarn as a valid trade and took pictures of Marion for them. They sneaked back into the designated area, pictures in hand. They hid the pictures away, saving them as a Hanukkah gift, and life continued.

OLD TROUBLES AS NEW

Hongkew, already full of people, quickly became overcrowded, with some larger rooms housing as many as sixty people. The overcrowding was exacerbated by the fact that the Japanese did not insist on the host of Chinese and Japanese residents moving out of the designated area, and most of them seemed uninterested in uprooting themselves for no good end. Hongkew had been the relatively inexpensive part of Shanghai to live in after its destruction, and many of the Chinese people who settled there did so because of costs. Moving elsewhere was not really an option for them.

Shortly after the other refugees moved into Hongkew, disease, always a problem in the tropical climate, became catastrophic in the overcrowding. A host of diseases swept through the ghetto, and since many of the refugees had already suffered malnutrition, diseases like measles became life threatening.

One of the diseases that had been making the rounds was diphtheria. This time around the girls in the Isaack family all contracted it. The refugee doctors were able and knowledgeable, but medicine was in short supply, again made worse by the hostility with the Western nations. What could be done for the girls was done, and both Lilly and Ingrid, with their age, had the stamina to withstand the disease. Marion—still a toddler, born into deprivation, and never having been properly nourished—did not. On December 14, 1943, at just over two years old, Marion passed away.

After much agonizing and letting Mr. Isaack in on the secret of their pictures, Ingrid and Lilly finally gave the pictures of Marion to Mrs. Isaack on Hanukkah as planned. While this created a whole new round of grief, it also gave Mrs. Isaack pictures of her baby-girl to treasure. Those pictures are still within the family and still treasured.

HOUSING IMPROVEMENTS AND WORSENING CONDITIONS

In Shanghai, most houses—particularly in row houses—had a meter room. This was a small room that housed the metering for the house or houses that it fed. While normally these rooms were used for things like storage, in the crowded environment of Hongkew, they increasingly became an extra room to be rented out for families to live in. They were always small and considered somewhat undesirable, because they averaged somewhere around one hundred square feet (9.3 sq. m). Yet they were small enough that only one family normally lived in them, making them attractive to anyone who valued privacy, which by this point was most of the refugees.

One day, Mr. Isaack came home to announce that while their arrangement with but one other family had been nice, he had secured a meter room for the Isaacks to live in. One more time they packed what little they had and moved. This room holds fond memories for Lilly, not for its grandness but for the privacy it offered the family and the intimate closeness that it enforced. In so small a space, a more fractious family may have had issues, but for the Isaacks, it was the best solution available.

As 1943 rolled into 1944, a growing number of refugees needed assistance. It was simply not possible to maintain a thriving economy in a small area of a city, and jobs were few, money scarce, and outside resources increasingly limited. The children were allowed to attend school outside the ghetto, but adults required the dreaded pass.

PASSES—OR THE LACK THEREOF

There were actually two people who issued passes to refugees. Goya was in charge of longer passes—a month and longer—while Okhura was in charge of very short-term passes, those issued for a week or less. Goya was an erratic man, who would ask children who was king of the Jews and then reward them with candy if they replied that he was or would jump up on his desk to slap tall refugees seeking passes. This official was very unpopular with the refugees, and his issuance of passes was best described as erratic. At one point, Mr. Isaack took young Joe aside and told him very clearly not to antagonize the man. It would seem that this advice was sound. Goya gave or denied passes at his whim, and he confiscated passes when irritated. His long-term Jewish secretary claimed that pass issuance was based more on his mood than on the actual reasons the refugee presented.

And yet the refugees seem to know Goya much more than Okhura, and far more long-term passes seem to have been sought than short-term passes. Common belief holds that this is because Okhura treated his position much more like a military position and was harsh in awarding passes at all, combined with the fact that Okhura was responsible for punishment of those who violated the pass system. Goya threatened to shoot people and had the authority to lock people in a disease-ridden jail, yet Okhura actually did these things while Goya merely threatened. Thus, one three-month pass from Goya was preferable to several day passes over the course of three months from Okhura, who was viewed as more harsh, even if more predictable.

Even though food was short in all of Shanghai due to overpopulation and war, there was even less food available in the Hongkew ghetto. People leaving Hongkew on a pass were one of the ways that extra food made it to the designated area. The erratic nature of Goya's pass issuance caused problems not just for that person but for his or her entire family and often for others.

The Japanese were not cruel to the refugees and did help the aid societies with food, but as the war went on, resources became strained for the Japanese also. The result of this was an ever-decreasing amount and quality of food. As Japan lost its possessions across Asia, their ability to help the refugee aid associations decreased, and food became nearly nonexistent. Moldy, bug-ridden bread and gruel became the food that most in the ghetto lived off. Writings of most refugees talk of it and of scraping off the bugs to eat the food. Lilly has these memories also, and it is difficult to convey in writing what her memory holds clear: things were bad in the ghetto and getting worse.

This was a low point for the refugees in terms of food. Shipments from the allies were stopped, exacerbating the already-troublesome food situation. Many refugees remember the food of this time, and none of them with relish. The Japanese authorities helped with food, but what this resulted in amounted to essentially moldy corn bread. To this day, the smell of cooking corn bread makes Lilly nauseous, and there are other people whose reaction is worse. There was enough food to survive, but barely, if you did not look closely at the food.

Mrs. Isaack taught the children to sleep on their stomachs so that the hunger pains would be less. The children, awakened to how their parents ate less and offered them the food intended for the adults, watched as their parents wasted away from a combination of recurrent disease and malnutrition. Whenever the children attempted to broach the subject, they were told that they needed the food to continue to focus at school. And, indeed, until the SJYA School was moved into the ghetto, the children were allowed passes to attend classes. The only real change to Lilly's school life was the addition of courses that the Japanese thought were essential. She was taught Japanese alongside English, Chinese, and German. Lilly remembers her time at school each day as an escape that allowed her to focus on something other than hunger and misery. And there was a meal provided at school, giving school-children more food than their adult counterparts.

FRIENDLY FIRE—LIFE WITH BOMBINGS

As the war ground on, and the allies came closer and closer to the Japanese home islands, bombing raids began to be a problem. Shanghai was not on the official bombing list at first, but it was designated a secondary target. Any plane that could not deliver its payload of high explosives to the primary target was allowed to drop on the secondary targets closest to their flight path. Shanghai was home to an ammo dump, an airport that housed Japanese military aircraft, and a wireless antenna serving Japan's mainland conquests. Several times, with increasing frequency, those targets were used—at first as secondary targets, when a plane had mechanical issues or a flight's primary target was too obscured by clouds to actually bomb, and later as primary targets, as the allies tried to deprive Japan of all military forces not within the home islands.

These Shanghai targets were regrettably close to Hongkew, and while it was not Allied military policy to bomb civilians who were not involved in the war effort, precision bombing simply did not occur from heavy bombers at high altitudes. While Allied bombers could bomb from extremely low altitudes (the Ploesti raiders flew just above treetop level, and D-Day B-24s dropped bombs from five hundred feet), they were built to bomb from high, and not terribly accurate, altitudes. The results in Hongkew were always bad and sometimes disastrous.

Existence in wartime Shanghai required a few familial arrangements that were not necessary in a more settled time and place. In one scenario, if things progressed to a certain point, the children were instructed to report to a specific pier on the Whangpoo River, and they would be met there and taken to safety. To this day, Lilly does not know who would have met them or where they would have been taken to, but she kept this information and would have gone, had her father said it was time. In another arrangement, if the bombing got too close and the home was in danger, any child at home was to gather the family's hoarded bag of dried bread that was their emergency ration and official papers and get out of the apartment, room, or home that they currently lived in.

One day (although Lilly does not remember clearly, this was likely July 22, 1944, the attack that in US military records is listed simply as "on Japanese positions"), while Lilly was home alone, a bomb fell upon the building across the street from their house. The building was utterly destroyed, and fire began. True to her instructions for the family's survival, Lilly snatched up the stash of dried bread, the family's papers, and, in a moment of thinking ahead, the family's coats. She wore one coat upon another to carry them, and in the stairwell outside their room, she discovered a kitten that looked every bit as scared as she was. Covered in layers of clothing, in a hurry to get away from the bombing, and carrying the family's meager cache of items necessary to survival, Lilly did what any young lady would do. She scooped up the kitten and placed it into her fathers' coat pocket and rushed on her way.

Lilly was so laden with the coats that she felt she could hardly move. As happens in high-tension situations, everything slowed for Lilly as she ran to the street, negotiated the rubble, and headed to reunite with her family. She was scared and alone, a girl in the heart of sudden destruction from the sky that cared not for the value of its victims and seemed outright capricious. But the bombing was limited, not the full-on attack that sometimes came, and Lilly was able to get to her family and hand over their jackets, the bag of bread, and their papers. Although it was a terrible moment in her life, Lilly still remembers the smile and joy that she felt as her father, having donned his coat, slipped his hand into his coat pocket to see what was in there and discovered her rescued kitten. The look on his face, rather than the terror that coexisted in that day, is what she chooses to remember.

As the war progressed, there were other bombings, some far more devastating than the one that had sent Lilly running from their home. Though they were lucky and were never caught directly in any of them, the bombing of July 17, 1945, stands out in the memories of most refugees, and Lilly remembers it still with a bit of terror mixed with awe. She and her sister were at school when it started. For an hour, heavy bombers delivered their payloads on Shanghai, presumably aiming for one of the military targets, but instead they dropped their bombs in the heart of Hongkew. The devastation was unparalleled in the experience of the refugees. While they had seen the destroyed wreckage of Hongkew when they had first arrived in Shanghai, this bombing took much that they had become accustomed to and turned it to rubble. Officially, the US Army Air Corps was attacking Jinghou airfield in Shanghai, which at that time held the largest concentration of Japanese military aircraft in mainland Asia. On both July 17 and 18, most of the bombs fell on Hongkew. On the seventeenth, most of the bombs fell on the area of Hongkew most heavily populated with refugees.

Lilly and her sister, Ingrid, were at school when the bombing started. As soon as they were allowed to get away, they rushed through the bombed-out remnants of the ghetto to find their family. Lilly remembers that the center of Hongkew was completely destroyed; "flattened" is the term she uses to refer to what they saw as they took to back roads and alleys, seeking a way through the destruction. The girls were forced to climb over or run around rubble that was often burning, negotiating their way through smoke and the remains of roads, trying to get to their parents.

Eventually Ingrid and Lilly did find their parents and brother, all miraculously unhurt.

While the various residents of Hongkew had learned during their enforced association to respect each other and even to get along, the July 17 bombing stands out, as the differences between people who did not even share a language were erased. Hundreds of both European and Chinese civilians were killed outright in the air raid, and many more were wounded. Doctors didn't care who you were or who they were; people ripped up their bedsheets for bandages and didn't wonder if it was going to their cousin or someone they could not even speak to; and ready hands dug through rubble, not caring if this block of row houses had held mostly Europeans or Chinese. In the midst of disaster, people did what good people have always done—helped those most in need. July 18 saw a follow-up bombing that also hit Hongkew, but it hit largely in the already-devastated area. Since people were prepared, there was less loss of life.

One of the many ways that Lilly remembers the terror of this bombing striking home to her personally was its impact on her friends. Several of her friends had been killed and wounded in the bombing, but most glaring in her memory is a young man named Moesche, whom the girls knew from school. He lost both of his parents in the bombing, and a few days later, they found him wandering the streets of the destroyed area, hopelessly looking for his lost parents. Lilly sometimes wonders what may have become of that young man, and she is well aware that only fate decreed that she not be in a similar situation in the course of that bombing raid.

As the allies planned for eliminating Japanese power outside their home islands, bombing of Shanghai military targets occurred with increasing frequency until the first atomic bomb was dropped on Japan, when bombing suddenly ceased. Few bombings produced significant damage, and Lilly remembers bomber awareness as a way of life.

Again Mr. and Mrs. Isaack's stability kept their children on an even keel. While Lilly heard from her friends how afraid their parents were of random bombing events, the Isaack children were grateful that their parents talked of Hawaii and how much better things would be in the future and taught them caution instead of fear.

THE END OF THE GHETTO

By the time of the bombing, the rats of Hongkew were starving. While humans can be counted on to observe certain niceties when hunger gnawed at their guts, animals cannot be counted on to do the same. Rats started attacking people in their sleep, and this caused people even more stress in an environment where neither stress nor nutrition levels were within healthy limits. One night a woman named Katz was attacked in her sleep and lost a toe to the hungry rodents. Those with any sense of humor remaining made the macabre joke that it was getting pretty bad when the rats were eating the Katz.

Throughout their time in the designated area, rumors of the end of the war would pass among the refugees. Time and again they proved to be only rumors, and yet they continued to circulate.

Eventually one of the rumors was close to the truth. The atomic bomb had been dropped, and the resulting cloud blocked the sun in Shanghai for days. Somehow the residents of Shanghai knew the truth, probably through clandestine radios. A group of young men banded together and went to the flagpole near headquarters, climbed up the pole, and replaced the Japanese flag with a Star of David flag. This presumably would be members of one of the Jewish youth associations, who would both have been forceful enough to decide such a task was a good idea and would have a Star of David flag ready-made for the occasion.

The Japanese guards rounded up the culprits, and though such disrespectful treatment of their authority was punishable by being shot on the spot, they merely told the boys to return the Japanese flag to the flagpole and that the war was not over until Commander Goya said it was over. Lilly remembers hearing her father discuss with her older brother, by now seventeen, that he should not be involved in such stunts and that it was both foolish and dangerous to risk one's life in a prank when merely waiting would see the results desired.

Eventually the rumor became official. The war was over. Lilly remembers that everyone—Chinese and the foreigners who lived with them, Russians, Turks, English, Americans, Germans, French, and, not to be left out, the Jewish people—danced into the night. After years of deprivation—for some, including prisons—only God will ever know how they found the strength to do that.

The Isaacks turned their minds to the same issues that most refugees suddenly freed in Shanghai did. They wondered what the future would hold, who of their family had survived the horrors of Europe after they left, how to contact any surviving family, and how they could improve their situation in the near term.

While they believed the worst was over, the refugees knew that they were not yet safe. In China, the nationalists and the communists were still fighting, and the refugees were still in a foreign land and needed to find a permanent place to live and a way to get there. Food was still hard to find, and all the survivors were very malnourished. Free they might be, but safe they were not.

AFTERMATH

Being aware of bombers was a way of life that never truly left Lilly, for later in life, aircraft flying too low over her house could automatically trigger internalized reactions such as slipping out of bed and rolling under it without thinking. Considering that this is true, one might wonder that her career choices after finally escaping Shanghai would include a stint in the newly formed US Air Force.

Food, also, created a long-term impact on Lilly. The smell of cooking corn bread makes her physically ill, even more than half a century after her Shanghai experience, and all food is well washed and well cooked. It is not a series of psychological problems that Lilly suffers but rather a set of learned behaviors that just are.

Cleanliness is also vital to Lilly. The type of cleanliness that most people do not require is a matter of course for her. Cleaning things that others might see as clean enough is one example of her overall tendency toward cleanliness. This is a logical outgrowth of living in conditions where the filth conducted wave after wave of disease and cleaning was but a temporary reprieve from overcrowding and tropical weather that turned streets into rivers.

And none of these things is disabling; indeed, all but a healthy fear of bombers flying overhead can easily be seen as benefits to a healthy lifestyle. And they are part of what makes Lilly herself.

Chapter 7

LOOKING FOR LIGHT
IN THE DARKNESS

Any community consisting of tens of thousands of people will have varia-tion in how those people deal with their situation in life. Whether in good times or bad, some will be lighter, perhaps even happy, while others are going to be morose or angry regardless of their surroundings. It is inevitable that harder times lend themselves to the darker side of the spectrum, but even so, the range covers happy to morose. In this, Shanghai was not unique.

PROFESSIONAL HELP

Where Shanghai may well have been unique in world history is in the number of professional entertainers that were included with the refugees. From op-era performers to comedians, Shanghai—specifically Hongkew—had more of them than most any comparable community. Many of Europe's greatest performers of the twenties and thirties had been Jewish. The same was true of Broadway at the time, but the entertainers on Broadway did not find them-selves needing to flee for their lives. Many of Europe's great performers ended up in Shanghai with their fellow refugees.

One of the performers who stuck with Lilly was Herbert Zernik, a famous comedian from Berlin. He had belonged to Berlin's Cabaret of Comedians before fleeing Germany. She remembers that whenever things got scary for the refugees, he would put on a free performance. She recalls that those performances gave people a break, the chance to forget about their troubles and to take a moment to laugh.

But Herr Zernik was not the only performer Lilly recalls.

Another group of refugees were opera performers. Lilly regularly went to dress rehearsals with a friend whose parents were involved in the opera group. Lilly says, "Without knowing it, they did more for the mood in the camps than they ever knew."

There were also cabaret performers. During the better times, they had played in clubs, and only those with spare money were able to attend. After refugees moved to the ghetto, the same groups put on shows for free in places that were accessible to anyone.

In the midst of crushing poverty, restricted movement, and forced relocation, these entertainers gave what they had for the benefit of everyone. While there has been no research into the impact this had on refugees, it no doubt contributed to a suicide rate that was much lower than to be expected (thirty-six total people of twenty thousand refugees in the years 1939–1945)[xi] for a people living in poverty and uncertainty.

Others did what they could also. Before the Japanese took over Shanghai, the JDC recruited a community-organizer husband-and-wife team to come from the United States and supported them in opening a youth center. They arranged for schools in the United States to exchange pen pals with the children in Shanghai's various Jewish schools. US schools sent over a cigar box—with toothpaste, toothbrush, comb, and so on—for children of the Shanghai Jewish School, and the boxes included the name of a pen pal. The children were thrilled with those boxes. Being so thrilled over so little is something that is difficult for modern people to understand. Goals were limited—stay alive and get out of China—so small things mattered more.

IT WAS PERSONAL, TOO

Life continues, whether it is harder or not. People are people, whether in need or not. Children are children, deprivation or not. Shanghai was no exception. Children found things to play with in the street, arranged games that did not require complex tools, and played pranks, just as they would in any other place.

Somewhere one of the other refugee girls found a partial box of pickup sticks that must have belonged to one of the younger children. She used these pickup sticks to teach several of the other girls how to knit with them although they were not exactly knitting needles. Clothes at the time could more easily be unraveled if they were patiently pulled apart. Lilly, her friends, and her sister unraveled clothes and put the strands freed together to make clothing. This didn't make perfect clothing, as the yarn had to be tied together in many places. Lilly remembers even today that "sitting on knitted panties is no joy when you have to sit in a classroom. The knots in our yarn were plentiful." Considering that they sat on a wooden bench, this no doubt is an understatement. But this exercise offered the girls a release.

Speaking of school, the children remained children although their circumstances were less than ideal. There is something about the mischievousness of those too young to admit that things are serious. While school was their release from the drudgery of the ghetto and the students learned much, they also practiced the same type of pranks that any other children in another school might have tried. For one teacher, they loosened the seat of the teacher's chair and put a bucket of water under it. When the teacher sat down, the seat gave way, and the teacher had a seat in the bucket.

Unlike most schools today, students stayed in a single room most of the day; the teachers changed classrooms unless the students went to a science lab. Once the students in Lilly's class tried putting a bucket of water over the door on the same teacher.

When the Isaacks moved into the room with but one other couple, it was at the Wayside camp. As much as their accommodations with one other family were enjoyable, the room tended to be hot and stuffy in the evenings, particularly in summer. Down the hall, there was a balcony that Mr. and Mrs. Isaack allowed the children to step out onto in the evenings to catch the breeze and cool down. The hallway to the balcony was lit by a single dim lightbulb—five watts or so.

One evening Lilly walked down the dim hall to find comfort from the oppressive heat of the summer night, and as she stepped out onto the balcony, something wet hit her face. Scared and uncertain about what had happened, she turned to go back inside. Mr. Isaack found her in the hall, covered in blood. While he was trying to calm her down and find the source of all the blood, Lilly's brother, Joe, came in from the balcony, laughing.

In the dark, he had thought the bucket was full of water. It was actually full of the ox blood used to paint the outside of buildings in Shanghai.

It was Lilly's only dress, and the ox blood had been out long enough to start to smell. Lilly was sent to bed while her mother found a way to clean the dress. Water at Wayside was not plentiful, so other families offered up their used washing water to help get first the blood and then the stains out of the dress. Meanwhile Lilly had to stay in bed, where her lack of clothes would be acceptable.

Her brother, of course, was in terrible trouble with their parents.

The last school prank we'll mention was more of a rite than a prank. The school had a real skeleton for teaching anatomy. The students made almost a game of trying to take a part of Seymore Bones home and bring it back without getting caught. Lilly stored a finger bone in her underwear drawer, no doubt worrying how her parents would react if it was found. The Isaacks felt that education was very important and did not tolerate foolishness where school was concerned. In the event, she was able to return the bone to Seymour Bones without getting caught.

In Shanghai of the late thirties and early forties, electric fuses were a piece of lead between two poles. When the fuse blew, someone had to take a strip of lead and insert it, getting shocked in the process. Once, while Mrs. Isaack was in the hospital with meningitis, Lilly's sister, Ingrid, was doing the ironing. The other children thought she ironed too much—it was probably a stress reliever—so as children do, Lilly put her hand on the ironing board to stop her. Ingrid finally put the iron on Lilly's hand. Needless to say, this stopped Lilly's interference. After that, the ironing blew one of the fuses. Ingrid told Joe, whose job would normally be to replace fuses, to replace the fuse. He was no more thrilled with the constant ironing than Lilly, so he told Ingrid, "You blew the fuse; you do it." Ingrid, being a loving big sister, turned to Lilly and told her to replace it. Learning a lesson that all younger siblings must learn eventually, that their siblings don't always have their best interests at heart, Lilly replaced the fuse and received the shock.

The war ended in August 1945, and Lilly's birthday was in September, just a month later. She got a pencil box with pencils, an eraser, and a sharpener. This gift, which most modern Western children would roll their eyes at, was perfect for her. When times are hard, it is the little things—the almost necessities but not quite—that are true gifts. The truth is that at least some of the reason for this gift was that the family had to find surviving relatives in a time when letters were the most reliable form of communication.

It was not just the children who found time for pranks, though. After the war, the Allies looked to the refugees to fill support roles that they needed. Many of the refugees spoke at least some English, and they knew the local area, making them the best possible employees. Before leaving Berlin, Mr. Isaack had been one of the few people in Europe with a car prior to the establishment of the Volkswagen. Because he knew how to drive, Mr. Isaack got a job with the Allies as a driver. One of the vehicles he drove was a two-and-a-half-ton six-by-six truck.

Recall that Lilly's uncle and aunt had come with them to Shanghai. Her uncle John did not have a job, but he did not know how to drive. Mr. Isaack taught Uncle John to drive in that two-and-a-half-ton truck, and Uncle John was hired also. One day, word came in that Uncle John would be transporting a truckload of Nazis, handcuffed and chained to the seats, to the pier in the back of his truck. They were to be returned to Germany to determine their involvement in the crimes of the Third Reich. The night before this transport was to take place, Mr. Isaack and Uncle John took the truck out and found the route to the pier with the most potholes along the way. The next day Uncle John drove them via that route and listened to the Germans in the back complaining about the stupid American who did not know how to drive. When they unloaded, he made it a point to thank them profusely in fluent German. While this was a small thing to offer to men who would have killed the refugees, Uncle John felt better knowing that he had got the message across. In his nineties, this story still amused him.

AND IT CROSSED BOUNDARIES

As mentioned elsewhere, the Chinese people were very accepting of the refugees, and Hongkew held more Chinese nationals than refugees. There were also, not incidentally, many Japanese families in Hongkew. These people mixed to make a community that shared hard times as the war dragged on, and even basic necessities became scarce for most of Shanghai. When bombings hit the civilian population, all fell out to restore order and see to the wounded. Chinese entertainers performed much as the refugee entertainers did and also did not charge. Although no one had much, those who had would help those who did not.

This even applied to some extent to the Japanese. A Japanese officer's wife sometimes took Lilly to a park by the river that was not normally accessible to refugees. They would go to the park, spend some time enjoying themselves, and return to the ghetto. One day they were walking into the park, but there were more guards than usual. The guards said something to the Japanese lady that Lilly did not understand; the children of the Shanghai Jewish School were taught Japanese, but they were speaking too fast for her. The lady took Lilly and told her that they could not visit the park today, and they returned without spending time in the park. Long after the war, Lilly learned that the park had been used for underground storage of ammunition, and she believes that they were building the bunkers when she and the Japanese lady were warned away. But the fond memory of the enemy's wife taking her to the park remains.

BUT, OF COURSE, IT WAS STILL COPING

No matter how well some deal with a bad situation, in the end it is still a bad situation, and given the chance, they will escape it, even if they managed to smile often while enduring. This was very much true of the refugee situation in Shanghai. Lilly's mother informed them repeatedly throughout their stay that no matter how bad things were, Shanghai was a safety net. As soon as the war was officially over, people began to make arrangements to get away. Very soon, shiploads of people were headed to Israel, and others were making their way as best they could to other countries that would take them. Having a good attitude is not the same as enjoying oneself. The Isaacks were not in these groups, as we shall see in coming chapters. But it is fitting to end this chapter with a preview of their eventual leave-taking with Lilly's thought as she looked over the stern of the ship that eventually took them away from Shanghai. She thought, *I'll probably never see that again, thank God.*

But she did see it again. Like other Shanghailanders, many years later, she felt the call to return and to see the city of her youth. But it was not seeing it again. It was visiting the memories, not living the reality.

Chapter 8

FREEDOM...OF SORTS

The war ended quietly in Shanghai. There were articles in refugee publications about two large bombs being dropped on Japan, and Lilly remembers the sky being overcast for days at a time. Then one night most of the Japanese guards were gone. There was no formal announcement, and there was no turning Shanghai over to the Allies; they just disappeared. For days, there was celebration in the streets. Slowly word spread that the war was indeed finally over. For people whose lives had been on hold for years—some for nearly a decade—this was jubilant news.

And the Americans came. Officially Shanghai was liberated by the Chinese Nationalist Army, but American troops were already there when the city was officially liberated. They found the state of the refugees and brought food. While things did not drastically improve, they were certainly better than they had been.

LEARNING OF EVENTS IN EUROPE
But the Americans had other news to share. The camps back in Europe had been found, and the Allies had video footage and pictures. The joy of being liberated gave way to fear for the fate of families. There had been persistent rumors, but now they were faced with the fact of genocide. And with the fact

of how successful that genocide was. The mood of refugees in Shanghai became somber, people discussing families and their discoveries more than their recently recovered freedom.

The Isaack family was no different than any other. They had left the majority of their extended family behind in Europe, and they now fretted over their fate. To find out how things stood, they, like so many others, wrote letters home and gathered around a message board where people posted any information they picked up in their own research.

It was soon obvious that their family had been decimated. It would be years before Lilly discovered that there were any survivors at all among those who had stayed in Europe.

But there was more to worry about than lost relatives. Now that they had freedom, they could travel to a land that was more settled. The Chinese were still in the middle of a civil war, and stability in the Shanghai region was questionable. Many of the refugees—those with family willing to sponsor them into other countries or, later, those willing to go to Israel—left as soon as that was possible.

There was also the issue of survival. Coming of the Americans brought food for the refugees, and aid again began to flow to Shanghai. But it would require money to get to another country, money for travel, for visas, for any number of incidental expenses.

And now that Shanghai was once again open to the refugees, they could look for better accommodations. While the *heime* had been a port in the storm of World War II, a place of their own away from Hongkew was important, now that it might be possible.

As mentioned earlier, Mr. Isaack used his knowledge of cars to get a job with the US troops driving a truck. This gave them a regular income and allowed them to start looking forward to moving.

At first Mr. Isaack's free time was spent learning about family in Europe, but eventually all resources and contacts eliminated, he was forced to admit that most of the family had perished. Thereafter, his free time was spent finding other ways to raise money to increase the funds they would have available to leave Shanghai.

FAMILY STOWAWAY

Shortly after the war ended, there was a bit of an interesting interlude. Lilly's brother, Joe, had grown to be a man while they were in the camp, and as a man, he decided he would take his chances trying to get out of Shanghai. By his reasoning, it was one fewer person for Mr. Isaack to worry about paying to get to their new home—wherever that home might be. Hoping to get to America, he stowed away on a cargo ship. He chose America because some family was already there. He was discovered when the ship stopped at Guam and was promptly placed on the next boat back to Shanghai. Lilly remembers there being heated words between her brother, Joe, and Mr. Isaack, but that is about all. Soon after Joe returned from his Guam adventure, Mr. Isaack arranged for him to travel to America legally in order to enter the country, sponsored by the relatives who were already there. His aunt and uncle were to be his legal guardians until he was twenty-one. Mr. and Mrs. Isaack made the difficult decision that they would split the family in a similar manner if it meant that they could get the other children out.

AMERICAN INVOLVEMENT

One memory Lilly carries of the early days of American occupation of Shanghai is of the sailors. As soon as the navy arrived in Shanghai, one of the primary concerns of the Allies was to take care of the refugee children. They would bus the children out to the pier, put them into little skiffs, and take them out to the troop ships. On the troop ships, the children were treated to a fun day with entertainment and a hearty meal. All the military personnel had been told not to feed these malnourished children anything except the food in the mess hall, since they had all been placed on various diets to recover from diseases and malnutrition.

Usually the last activity of the day was a movie. As soon as the lights went out, someone would whisper in a child's ear, "Take some and pass it on," and a big brown bag of all sorts of candy would be handed to the child. Whenever the child would look around to see who had given him or her this treasure, there was no one there. The children loved it, for they knew that they were getting away with something. It wasn't until many years later that Lilly would come to realize that these young men must have felt a very special compassion for the children in order to risk their rank and possibly even being sent to the brig. To this day after serving in the military herself, she hopes that all the sailors fared well and that none got into trouble on the children's account.

Once America understood the number of refugees in Shanghai and the perilous state of their existence, things began to move. Through aid societies, the US people had pulled together, and actual goods that were useful to the refugees' continued existence began to arrive. No doubt some of this high level of donations had much to do with the decimation of Europe's Jewish community. Those Jews living in Shanghai now represented a significant number of Holocaust survivors. So the aid societies sent what was needed—clothes, coats, enough food.

And with these things, the American military brought doctors to evaluate the refugees' health. After what was found in Europe, they feared the worst. And truly although the Japanese treated the refugees far better than the Nazis treated Europe's Jews, what the doctors found was bad enough. To use the example of Lilly's family, Mr. Isaack stood over six feet tall and weighed ninety-three pounds; Mrs. Isaack was just over four feet tall and weighed fifty pounds; Ingrid was fifty-one pounds; and Lilly herself was fourteen years old and weighed fifty-two pounds. Lilly's brother, Joe, was already on the boat to Guam when the doctors examined the family. The Isaacks were pretty average for the refugees, and truly the Chinese citizens of Shanghai were not much better off.

LIFE BEGINS TO NORMALIZE

Housing was still a problem for a variety of reasons. Most refugees stayed in their existing situation in Hongkew for a while. More of the Chinese people were being driven into the city by the civil war, swaths of the city were in ruins, and the arriving Allied troops needed a place to stay also. So housing was difficult to find.

Eventually Mr. Isaack found the family a one-bedroom apartment. After years of living with others and always in a single room, having an apartment with a bedroom, kitchen, and living room was heaven. Lilly's parents took the bedroom, and the two girls set up cots in the living room.

Mr. Isaack's demeanor began to change. After years of scraping along and not finding work because there was not any to be had, he was working for the Americans, driving trucks and buses. He had managed to get his family a place to live that was all for them. And he had sent his oldest child to a new life in a country that many of the refugees dreamed of. Always an optimistic and pleasant man, he now showed the self-possession that men who have known true deprivation feel when they are finally able to provide for their family.

Things were looking up for the Isaacks. They continued to spend time searching for family, and they planned and made arrangements to travel to America. Life began to seem normal.

Once again Mr. Isaack's sense of humor and responsibility for his children showed through. He came home from work one day to announce, "Once a month we will eat as we did during the war."

Clearly, he had not discussed this decision with Mrs. Isaack, because she asked, "And who is going to cook that?"

Mr. Isaack responded, "I will."

Mrs. Isaack's response was totally expected. "This, I have to see."

Lilly knew that Mr. Isaack couldn't cook. Couldn't even begin to cook. In her words, "Remember, this is a man who couldn't peel potatoes."

When the day arrived, Mr. Isaack went to the icebox, which was a luxury but was, of course, the old-fashioned version that actually used ice, and took out the items he would cook. The items he took out reflected what little they had eaten for years. He set the items on the table, and then he announced that the family would all dress in their best clothes and would be eating at Wing Gong. Wing Gong was a very elegant restaurant. They dressed in their finest and made their way to the restaurant, where they had a fine meal. Thereafter, once a month, the family went through the same ritual. In the long run, Mr. Isaack's intent was driven home. They remembered how hard things had been while they enjoyed that they no longer were. "Don't forget how bad things can be and can be survived" was one of his favorite phrases.

NORMALCY, PERSONIFIED

Things became very normal seeming. Things were still very much temporary, but the crushing poverty was largely lifted. Indeed, things became so normal that Mrs. Isaack became pregnant. While this was not an ideal time to have another child, it was certainly a better time than there had been in nearly a decade. Mr. Isaack was ecstatic, as if this child would be his firstborn. Mrs. Isaack was also very pleased. Their mood elevation was contagious, and the girls picked it up also. There was enough money to buy a crib, and Lilly's sister, Ingrid, painted Mickey and Minnie Mouse on the headboard. While the new baby would have to sleep in the room with Mr. and Mrs. Isaack, they were used to sleeping in rooms overflowing with people, so one baby was not much of an imposition.

The only negative to the pregnancy was how soon it came after famine. The doctors advised Mrs. Isaack that she should not go through with the pregnancy, but there was little chance that either she or Mr. Isaack would agree to that idea. The doctors' primary goal was to keep Mrs. Isaack alive. It was only ten months after she had been weighed by American doctors and had come in at fifty pounds, and now a child would get its nutrition from her. She was also thirty-nine years old, which complicated the pregnancy. It was a difficult nine months for Mrs. Isaack.

When finally the day came and Mr. Isaack came to take Mrs. Isaack to the hospital, he was nervous—also as if this were his first child. He could hardly tell the rickshaw driver where to go. He was gone for many hours, but when he returned, Lilly remembers that at first he looked like it was he who had delivered his new son. He came home to announce that the children had a brother: Fred H. Isaack. As he calmed down, he was elated. As Lilly says, "You would think he was Adam, and Fred was the first child ever born."

The Isaacks in 1947, Shanghai

With their increased money, the girls' education was advanced. Ingrid was sent to an art school, while Lilly stayed at the Shanghai Jewish Youth Association School but was placed in a track for those headed into medicine. In those days, the parents chose children's profession, and Lilly's parents were against her going into medicine. Mr. Isaack thought it would be too strenuous for a woman. They wanted her to be a secretary. But the tenacity that comes from her heritage and the environment she grew up in showed through, and Lilly used that tenacity to convince them that this was the right choice for her.

The girls were starting to consider their futures.

But fate was not done with the Isaack family or indeed with many of the refugees.

The nationalist Chinese government was in trouble. It was basically an alliance of warlords, and it was losing battles to the Red Chinese. Lost battles often lost supporters also. As the area controlled by the government shrank and it was seen internationally as prosecuting the war poorly, the revenues—in both actual income and the ability to borrow from other countries—shrank precipitously. The government needed money to pay their warlords and to continue to otherwise function, so it did what too many governments do in such situations. It printed more money.

Soon the residents of Shanghai noticed that there was inflation. Worse, the government's plan was to continue printing money to pay its bills, meaning that the inflation would get worse.

The money Mr. Isaack was earning working for the Americans was not going as far, and things were getting tight again. As many other residents of Shanghai did, Mr. and Mrs. Isaack began buying gold on the black market. It was illegal for individuals to own gold in China, so there was a risk. The prices of gold were also artificially inflated, but gold generally retained its value, no matter what happened to the currency.

Eventually the Isaack girls would go to the market with a basketful of money and return with hardly any groceries. Hard times were back, with only the gold buffer keeping the Isaacks comfortable.

Meanwhile, the paper work to move any of them out of the country was endless. As the Isaacks were stateless persons, there was no one to check with about the refugees and their backgrounds. The Isaacks had targeted either the United States or Australia as where they would try to go, but emigration to any country was difficult for stateless people. They didn't even have proof that they had been born, since the Nazi government had only allowed them to take their passports. They required passports, visas, sponsors, a quota number, and, most importantly, time. Time to arrange for some form of most of these items and time for their quota number to arrive. Mr. and Mrs. Isaack worked the system while casting about for any way to get the children out of the country.

It should be noted here that by now, Western governments were acting in favor of the refugees. It is just that they were not acting forcefully enough. Or more to the point, they wanted others to take in the thousands of refugees. Most country's records are still not public, but the United States has published internal communications between ambassadors and Allied governments. It is unfortunate that the United States wanted other countries to take the refugees, and other countries most often responded with suggestions that someone else take them. No matter which Allied government the communications dealt with, all read as if they care and know that the refugees needed to be taken care of, but only Israel (once it was a country in 1948) stood up and started taking refugees as soon as possible.

Meanwhile the search for surviving family continued. In 1947, the Isaacks found a younger relative who had survived the Holocaust and asked her to check on the status of Mrs. Isaack's parents in Berlin. While Mrs. Isaack's family was not Jewish, the impact of the war on civilians living all over Europe was known to the refugee community. The young woman traveled to Berlin and discovered that their building was one of the few surviving on the street. She went to the door of the apartment where Mrs. Isaack's parents had lived in before the war and found both of Lilly's maternal grandparents alive.

This was the first close family that they had managed to find alive, and it would be the last. Slowly the other results also came in. After the war, Lilly's uncle was returning from the Eastern Front, where he had served with the German army, and as the former German soldiers exited the train, Russian soldiers shot them all dead. Most of the family had been sent to concentration camps and never returned. Lilly's paternal grandmother, for example, was known to have been taken to Buchenwald, but there the trail ran cold. There was very little left for the Isaacks in Europe; their world had been decimated.

As time passed, the refugees in general, and the Isaacks in particular, started to look more normal as they put on some of the lost weight.

Meanwhile the red tape trickled on. Lilly remembers many trips to the American consulate, several physicals, all in an attempt to get approval to enter the United States.

The communists were clearly winning the Chinese civil war and were approaching closer and closer to Shanghai. Due to communist influence, the Chinese people, who had generally been accepting and helpful to the refugees through all the previous years, started to treat the refugees differently. The Americans were interested in the refugee community for a variety of reasons, from the fact that the refugees generally spoke English to the fact that they were some of the few survivors of the Holocaust. In fact, the only complete ye-shiva (roughly, an orthodox Jewish seminary) from Europe was in Shanghai, so thorough was the destruction of Judaism in Europe.

While the reasons for American interest in the refugees were valid, these people who had no country and were struggling to gain entrance into America found themselves the recipients of statements like "Yankee, go home." That was the beginning of an increasing—although not yet violent—animosity from the Chinese people.

FATE'S FINAL BLOW

After all that fate had dealt to the Isaacks, it held one last devastating blow for the family. On August 12, 1948, Mr. Isaack was found in the hold of a ship. His heart was still beating, but his head was compressed down to four inches. He died within hours.

Mrs. Isaack did not speak English. She had three underage children in a country torn by the worst kind of war—a civil war. She was struggling to get them all out of the country. And she was suddenly alone.

No one knows how Mr. Isaack ended up in the hold of a ship with his head crushed. Trading gold in the black market held an element of danger, as did working for the Allies. But the police came to Mrs. Isaack and explained that it could be reported as an accident or a homicide. If it was a murder, then the family had to stay in Shanghai until the investigation was complete.

This small woman not known for her strength made the only logical decision. She told them to file it as an accident. She took the time to explain to the
children that Mr. Isaack wanted nothing more than to get them all to safety
and that, no matter how it was reported, it would not bring the children's
father back. They had to keep on living; it was what he would want.

Mr. Isaack had always been late, no matter the appointment. It was a
common thing for Mrs. Isaack to tell him, "Kurt, you will be late for your
own funeral." Little did she know that her quip would be prophetic. The
day of his funeral arrived, and the weather had turned to the type of driving
rain that mainland Asia sees in August. Everyone was standing in the rain,
waiting for the casket, but there was no sight of the bearers and their burden.
The rabbi became agitated, and still there was no sign of Mr. Isaack's casket. Finally, about twenty minutes late, the bearers showed up. It turned out
that the Jewish tradition of walking the casket past the earthly abode of the
deceased had caused the bearers to get turned around and lost on the wrong
street; they had been forced to backtrack and then find their way to the funeral. So as a last jest, Mr. Isaack was indeed late for his own funeral.

While the family was at the funeral, thieves broke into their apartment
and helped themselves to the Isaacks' secret stash of gold. So now Mrs. Isaack
had another thing to contend with. The money they had been saving to escape the country was also gone now.

This was no doubt the low point for the Isaack family. But many Jewish
communities are tight-knit, and while the Shanghai Jewish community had
divisions, their shared loss and hardship had bonded them like few others.
Shortly after the funeral, food and some money were arranged for the Isaacks.
Since the girls were in school, Fred was too small to earn money, and Mrs.
Isaack needed to be there for the family and could not work, this lifeline was
sorely needed.

While the bulk of the Chinese people were still warm and welcoming
to the refugees, communist agitators were raising tensions with some of the
more brash, particularly among the youth. From saying, "Yankee, go home!"
they started throwing things—vegetables, feces, and sometimes even rocks—
at the refugees. It soon got bad enough that the inside of the windows had to

be covered so that a rock breaking the window would not send shards of glass around the room and hurt someone.

Since they had no money and no reliable way to get more, Mrs. Isaack let Santia, their Chinese housekeeper, go. Even though the woman was no longer in Mrs. Isaack's employ, she still came and did the shopping for the family to keep the Isaacks off the street and relatively out of harm's way.

THEN CAME THE END

Since 1947, US troop ships had been used to transport refugees who had been granted entry into another country as their new home. In 1948, America passed the Displaced Persons Act, authorizing nearly two hundred thousand people displaced during World War II to enter the United States, provided they met certain criteria. The Shanghai refugees were targeted to be part of that influx of displaced persons.

As the nationalist government began to collapse and the Chinese Peoples' Liberation Army (the military branch of the Chinese Communist government) closed in on Shanghai, America decided that it was time to act more strenuously than they had been doing. All refugees (and some White Russians and Poles who were not displaced by World War II) who had valid entry papers for another country were to be removed from Shanghai.

As 1948 came to a close, the Isaacks learned that they were approved for entrance into the United States and that transport would be provided on one of the troop ships. Finally, after so many things had happened, they were to be on their way to a new home. Dealing with American troops, hearing them talk of home, and getting what seemed an unending supply of food from the US Navy, the refugees held a belief that America truly was the promised land. But honestly it was a safe haven; there is little doubt that they would have gone even without the rumors.

Finally, they were set to leave in February 1949. The night before they were to leave, Lilly was awakened by Santia (their erstwhile maid), who had a shovel. After waking Lilly, she instructed the girl to hurry and get dressed so that they could go get Lilly's papa. After some exchange that Lilly remembers as being rather surreal, she told Santia, "We just put him in the ground, and he's just going to have to stay there; he will not go to America, except in our hearts." Lilly believes that Santia looked relieved as she nodded her understanding and promised to go and talk to Lilly's papa once in a while.

That was early morning, before sunrise. But Lilly was now awake and on the day that they would leave on another great adventure. She stayed up until the bus came to take them to the pier. At the pier, they were placed upon a PT boat and transported to the SS *Gordon*.

Lilly remembers standing at the railing, looking at Shanghai, and being full of terribly mixed emotions. Everything she had known in her life was being left behind. She had been in Shanghai since she was six years old, and now she was a young lady. But she was also elated at the thought that there was a life for her out there, that she would not live and grow old struggling in Shanghai. As China faded into the distance, a young sailor came alongside of her and started to talk of the many possibilities for her in the United States. He said that he had a sister who was about her age and that the girl was going to high school, and he talked about the prom that she attended. He showed Lilly a picture of his sister in her prom dress; she was lovely. Lilly admired that girl whom she didn't even know.

But the future was ahead, and Shanghai was finally as behind as it could be.

Chapter 9

ANOTHER STRANGE NEW LAND

Leaving Shanghai was a bit of a scary ending for Lilly and the others on the SS *Gordon*, but it was also a new brave new beginning. She had gone to Shanghai at age six, and here she was at sixteen, setting off to America, the land that she had heard stories of that seemed unbelievable. She quickly learned that there was much she did not know. The sailors spoke like they had a hot potato in their mouths and used words she was unfamiliar with. She had been educated in English, but the Queen's English, and that in an educational setting. Doubts still assailed Lilly, but that ship had sailed. Her life lay ahead, and she needed to learn.

The sailors went out of their way to make the refugees feel welcome and safe. The sailors saw to it that they had the comforts of home, as far as that was possible on a ship. They brought the Isaack children candy bars and took little Freddie to get ice cream so that the Isaack women could sneak away to catch a movie. One of Lilly's strongest memories is of the sailors. After years of varying levels of deprivation, being treated like human beings left a strong impression on Lilly, one of regard for American GIs. Technically the crew of the SS *Gordon* were merchant marines, as the ship had been transferred to the American President Line after World War II. But it is a safe bet that each sailor aboard was former US Navy, since World War II had inducted so many sailors.

FINALLY AMERICAN SOIL

After twenty days on the ocean, they came to Hawaii. This was a bittersweet moment for the Isaack family, for all remembered Mr. Isaack's jokes about going to Hawaii and finding a hula-hula girl for him and a hula-hula boy for Mrs. Isaack. He had so wanted to arrive in Hawaii, and here they were without him.

While adjusting to the sailors was a beginning, Honolulu offered an entire society of difference for the Isaacks to explore. They were only in Hawaii for a short time, but they took the opportunity to see all that they could.

It was in Hawaii that Mrs. Isaack taught the girls to learn acceptable behavior by sitting back and watching others interact. "We learn by watching," Mrs. Isaack told them. Lilly took this to heart and learned many social mores by watching and listening to those around her interact.

But first they had to get through customs. Mrs. Isaack only had one copy of Fred's birth certificate remaining, and their very first encounter with an American customs official saw a demand that she hand it over.

Mrs. Isaack did not speak English, so through Lilly and Ingrid, she was told that she must turn it over and that it would be returned when they entered the mainland. With some trepidation, she produced the birth certificate and handed it to the customs official. That was the last that they heard of that birth certificate. Not until after serving in the US Army and living his entire life in America did Fred manage to get a copy of his own birth certificate although he tried to obtain a copy many times before successfully obtaining one.

By the number of people who asked her where she was from, Lilly quickly realized that she sounded as odd to others as they sounded to her, and she set her mind to improving her English. Talking to her today, you can barely hear the odd mix of her accent, and it is definitely not identifiable—being a mix of German, Chinese, and Queen's English.

Food markets in Shanghai were all open-air affairs, and due to the slaughtering of animals right there in the market, they always smelled horrible. So it was with some trepidation that the family went to an indoor market (a supermarket) to find some food. They were pleasantly surprised at the lack of smell, the cleanliness, and the way that the food was presented. But in Shanghai, there was always someone there to take care of customers' needs, and here they were standing in the produce section, waiting for someone to arrive and help them pick out food. When no one came to help them, Lilly took to watching what other people were doing. People would pick out their own food and take it to the front, where a cashier would check them out, and they would pay. This was completely different than Shanghai, but they picked up some bananas and went to a cashier, paying and receiving change.

This is when they noticed something odd that is still true today, but people born and raised in America wouldn't notice. In their change, there was a dime. The coin does not indicate its value anywhere on it. Where it might say, "Ten cents," it instead says, "One dime." This caused some confusion as the Isaacks figured out what the value of a dime was.

Soon enough, they were back on the SS *Gordon* and on their way to San Francisco. Finally, they would arrive in their new home.

Leaving Hawaii was the signal for Lilly's sense of adventure to kick in. But it wasn't just Lilly. The next few days, the excitement and anticipation among the refugees in general grew. Finally, they would be at their destination, although for some aboard the SS *Gordon*, it would not be their final destination. Some were being granted transit through the United States to Newark, and from Newark, they would be put on a ship to head to Israel. Yet those whose ultimate destination was Israel shared the excitement of being somewhere that wasn't on the edge of hostility toward them.

Just a side note about those who were only crossing the United States to board a ship bound for another country. These people, after all their suffering, were put on sealed trains with armed guards. They were not allowed off the trains at any point in America, and they traveled across the country at a train's pace without seeing anything more than they could glimpse out the window. The reasoning of the US government was that these people were not cleared for American citizenship and could not be allowed to slip off into the populace. But it must have felt strange to them that the country they viewed as saviors viewed them as a security risk.

MAINLAND AMERICA—FIRST IMPRESSIONS

The ship approached the coastline at three in the morning, and Lilly remembers that all the refugees were on the deck to see America. They had waited a long time for this moment. To this day, Lilly remembers that seeing San Francisco for the first time was "awesome," as it represented their freedom. This is normally where words fail Lilly, and she simply says, "It was a feeling you cannot describe." As the SS *Gordon* passed under the Golden Gate Bridge, a hush fell over the deck. The bridge was lit, as though it were saying, "Welcome to my country and to freedom!" On the right, the warm glow of San Francisco's lights illuminated sky and shore, and Lilly remembers that it looked like the entire town was saying, "Welcome," just to her. She cried a little, not knowing exactly why. Was it happiness, sadness for all she never had, or just relief, knowing things would finally work out? She did not know.

This was the first moment in her life that Lilly truly felt there was a tomorrow to look forward to. There was. In fact, there were many.

The Isaacks went down the ramp to the pier, and Lilly remembers taking a deep breath and thinking, *America, here I come.* But before America, there was customs. The line was very long, and dealing with refugees made it particularly slow. Some spoke little English. What they had to declare varied based upon what they had to bring along, and none of them understood what would be required of them.

So Lilly and Ingrid took turns standing in line with their mother and watching their brother, and the one who did not have Fred in hand would try different vantage points to see if she could spot their uncle John and aunt Harriet, who lived in California (having come two years earlier), and who had agreed to meet them at the pier.

Eventually their turn came with the customs officials, and America would show just how welcoming a country it was. When asked how much money she had, Mrs. Isaack (translated by her daughters) told them $26.50. The customs official looked at her, looked at her children, and said quietly, "I'm going to adjust that number. No one will believe a widow traveled across the world with three children and only twenty-six dollars and fifty cents, and they will detain you, searching your things for more money." He wrote down, "$265.00." Mrs. Isaack thanked the agent, and they were on their way.

One thing they did require of the refugees was to sign a document that agreed if they were ever convicted of a crime or found themselves on welfare, they would be deported. To this day, Lilly does not know where, exactly, you would deport a stateless person to. America had struggled with the Displaced Persons Act, and no doubt this document was to allay some of the concerns of those opposed to the law. We cannot know about all refugees, but Lilly took this requirement to heart. She was being handed a whole new life; "don't commit crime" and "don't be on welfare" seemed like a bargain to her.

They were finally well and truly in America. Neither Mrs. Isaack nor Fred spoke a word of English, but with Ingrid and Lilly to translate, they did well enough and were starting to learn some of the colloquialisms (though certainly not all of them, as we shall see). Consequently, they were not terribly handicapped by the language barrier.

Uncle John and Aunt Harriet were there waiting for them, along with two of Aunt Harriet's nephews who had also come to America about two years earlier, and their first miniature reunion was held. The Jewish refugee organization HIAS had already made arrangements for the Isaacks to stay at a hotel and to provide for dinner with their family. The first day in America was practically a life of luxury. They went to an amusement park, and Lilly remembers being awed by the experience. Everyone they met seemed so nice, seeming to bend over backward to be kind to them. Already America felt a little like home.

They spent a total of five days in San Francisco before they were on their way to New Jersey and their final home. Lilly's uncle Heinz and aunt Kate (who had sponsored Joe when arrangements were made for him to leave in 1947) were to be legally responsible for them, since they were stateless persons, so they were traveling to live near Aunt Kate in New Jersey.

LISA MAC VITTIE WITH DONALD W MAC VITTIE

HEBREW INTERNATIONAL AID SOCIETY (HIAS)

As HIAS had arranged for their food on the train and they had sleeping compartments, the three days of travel were relatively stress-free. The girls watched what was going by, getting a glimpse of the country coast to coast. While they were watching out the windows, though, a colloquialism they did not yet understand became apparent. The train passed many signs that said, "Lots for sale." It puzzled them throughout the trip, for they could not figure out what was being sold. Clearly lots of it was being sold, so it must be common. Yet the signs never indicated lots of *what*.

All that HIAS had done for them would be hard to list here, but as an example, when the train pulled into Chicago, they were met by a woman who asked if they were the Isaack family. When they replied that they were, she asked them to come with her and took them to a cab. The faith that Mrs. Isaack must have had in the world (or in Americans) is amazing to pull into a strange city, be met by a stranger, and allow her family to be taken to a car to be transported...somewhere. Lilly believes that it was faith in humanity and God both that allowed Mrs. Isaack to trust at this point in her life. It was wise to send a female cab driver, though; whoever was in charge of that transfer was thinking. The lady took them to another train station and got them on the train from Chicago to Newark, their final destination.

NEWARK—A NEW HOME

Arriving in Newark, they were met off the train by Lilly's *tante* (aunt) Kate and *onkel* (uncle) Heinz, along with their son, Warren. It had been ten years since she'd seen them, but in the manner of all younger people, she was surprised that they looked older. Warren, who had been a baby when she'd last seen him, was even in a Boy Scout uniform. Lilly had lived through ten years that varied from inconvenient to downright hostile, and yet she did not connect that time to her family. Needless to say, this reunion was sweet. As she observes today, it was almost as if she'd not looked in a mirror and seen her own growth over the last decade.

Lilly's brother Joe was at work, but he joined them that evening for dinner. Yet another reunion was enjoyed in a place of relative safety. This first evening was also when they discussed employment possibilities and familial responsibilities so that they could all survive in their new home.

When they had left Shanghai, they left much as they had come—with a suitcase each and in clothes from Shanghai that had been mended or were lower quality due to conditions in Shanghai. Lilly's tante Kate took the girls in hand and took them to a department store. The impression of a US department store was so strong that even decades later, Lilly would remember the name: Bambergers. This turned into a marathon shopping event, as Ingrid and Lilly wanted to look at everything in the store in addition to needing clothing and underclothing from head to toe. But Tante Kate wanted them to fit in, and she managed them like a champ, dressing them in the fashions popular among American girls at the time.

Meanwhile Uncle Heinz found two rooms to rent for them, which was probably oddly comforting after their recent living arrangements. Something larger might have been discomfiting for a first place to stay in this strange land.

Uncle Heinz was a teacher, so he made arrangements for Lilly to be tested for placement in the school system. It is a testament to the Shanghai Jewish School and her parents that Lilly tested post–senior level. But the communications barrier did offer a bit of a problem when the results were presented. When it was announced that she had the equivalent of eighteen years of school, Lilly forcefully informed her testers that the result was obviously wrong—indeed it was impossible—since she was only sixteen years old. The room got a chuckle out of this, but it took her a while to figure out what was so funny. No doubt this continued to offer a chuckle for those teachers for many years. Once that misunderstanding was cleared up, the decision was made to put Lilly in the senior class and to let her walk with her class in 1949. Due to the short amount of time she spent in American schools, Lilly was not allowed to graduate, but she was allowed to walk with the class.

Because her time in high school was short, Lilly has few memories of an American high school, but she does recall learning about combination locks and the way they worked on the first day. She also recalls one of her first interactions with students. They had announced that a new girl coming from China would be joining the class. She overheard one girl say to another, "I wonder if her eyes will slant up or down?" Lilly quipped, "Why don't you turn around and look. I never was able to determine that myself." Thus started one of her first friendships in high school.

Lilly's aspirations were to be a doctor, but there were several barriers to this dream. First was her age. Even today age can be a barrier to college admission, but in 1950, it was a larger issue. Second was gender. America was going through a sort of miniature equal-rights movement after World War II had introduced the likes of Rosy the Riveter, but the key word is "miniature." There was a general resistance to female attendance at university, and that resistance increased for postgraduate studies. Had those been the only issues, Lilly probably would have climbed the mountain and followed her dream. But the biggest hurdle was financial. College was expensive for anyone, but it was totally out of reach for someone who was recently essentially broke and had no income. Complicating the cost was family situation. Mrs. Isaack could not speak English and thus could not find a job that made enough to cover the expense of day care for Freddy. She needed help, and the girls were the logical source of that help. While Lilly's uncle and aunt were happily providing support, Mrs. Isaack and the girls did not want to be a burden, and strove for financial independence.

Ingrid's first job was at a bakery, and the family was once again convinced of the goodness held in American hearts, when the owner of the bakery told her to take home what her family could eat from the day-old baked goods. What she didn't take home to the family was sold at a discount, but the Isaack family did not have to pay. They were grateful for the help.

Lilly took jobs here and there to help support the family, and then she was lucky enough to land a position at RCA Victor. RCA of the 1950s was a company that invested heavily in their employees, and Lilly took advantage of this fact. She took classes while working. If a class had to be taken during the day, she had but to give them advanced warning, and they were happy to put her on the night shift for the duration of the class. All the while, they were paying her more than most men made at the time. Lilly stayed with RCA Victor for five years, but there was always something more she wanted to do.

American soldiers had given their lives to save her and other Jews across the world. America, once it had thrown itself into the war, gave unselfishly both at home and on the battlefield. With America as the armory of the free world, the Allies had, at great expense, defeated Nazis and the imperial Japanese and made the world free again. Perhaps more importantly, America had given Lilly a home when her own country had revoked her citizenship simply because of who she was. And it had not just given her a home; when the country accepted the refugees, Americans overall welcomed them. In her own words, Lilly could not replace the lives that had been lost for her; she had taken so much and had so little to give in return.

She joined the Civil Air Patrol, thinking that might be a small bit she could pay back to America—and apparently not thinking that a full-time job plus college might be busy enough. This time with the Civil Air Patrol exposed Lilly to the US Air Force.

On November 11, 1954, Lilly achieved citizenship. She took the oath of citizenship and finally had a country that was her own again. Since she was six when her former country had removed her citizenship, America was her first real country.

Chapter 10

FINALLY A HOMELAND

Shortly after Lilly took her oath of citizenship, she went to the Air Force recruitment office and signed up to do what she could to pay back the debt she felt she owed America. Here she ran into another unanticipated problem. Her lack of a high-school diploma meant that she was not qualified to enter the Air Force. The Air Force, upon learning of her story and knowing how her academic testing showed her progress, was willing to make an exception—if she could get a letter from her Shanghai school that attested to her academic ability.

This was not a simple problem to tackle. Communist Chinese had taken over Shanghai, and even if the Shanghai Jewish Youth Association School was still open, Western communications with anyone in China were difficult. There was one slim hope that Lilly could think of. She knew where one of the instructors from the SJYA School lived in the United States. Unfortunately, that teacher was the one who disliked her, Ms. Lesser.

Lilly wrote Ms. Lesser and asked for the required letter. Remembering Ms. Lesser's animosity, she waited with concern, but eventually the letter came. Ms. Lesser gave her the required documentation: testament that she had completed form six, the equivalent of the last year of high school. With Ms. Lesser's letter, Lilly's goal of joining the US Air Force moved forward.

In December 1954, she enlisted in the Air Force. When an officer welcomed her, the Air Force had abbreviated her name from Liselotte Isaack to L. ISA, and a drill instructor dubbed her "Lisa." That became her name in the Air Force, and in the long run, that is the name she chose to be known by in the United States. Because she is known as Lisa in the United States, that is the name we will use for the rest of this book.

Basic training for women was still a growing phenomenon in the 1950s; the WAF was only founded in 1948 and had been extremely limited. As women proved their success in the roles allowed them, the number of roles—and the number of women accepted—grew. Because of this growth, there were plenty of opportunities for drill instructors. Thus it was that Lisa eventually found herself as a Drill Instructor at Lackland Air Force Base.

A Match Made in Heaven

Lisa and Mac on their wedding day. Photo credit: *Air Force Times*

There she met another drill instructor, Herbert "Mac" Mac Vittie. He was a man who brought levity to nearly every situation, and soon they were fast in love. He proposed on Halloween, a fact that some might view to be apropos, given he had an irrepressible sense of humor.

Soon they were the first couple to marry where both spouses were active-duty Air Force. Things were slowly changing in the Air Force, and no one asked Lisa to resign. But American society in general and the Air Force in particular were not totally changed, so eventually she would be asked to leave—though not because of the wedding.

Lisa went home on leave to inform her mother that she'd met the man of her dreams and that she was married. While she was home, representatives of the German government came to inform them that Germany would be paying restitution. Mrs. Isaack was working by this time but certainly not thriving, so it shows the spunk that she had exhibited throughout the war when she insisted that she did not want their blood money. Eventually with Lisa's help, they convinced her that all she had lost did deserve some reparations, even if she gave it to a charity, but it was a slow process.

As happens with newlyweds, Lisa was soon pregnant. At the time, the Air Force believed that a mother needed to focus on being a mother, not on being a service member, and this was the event that triggered the end of her service. But this did not get Lisa down; she did have a family to plan, and things were changing for the Mac Vitties.

RETURN TO GERMANY

Mac received an assignment to Germany. Of all the possible duty stations that they could be sent to, Germany had to come up. Lisa spoke German, but the last time she was there, she had run for her life.

This entire situation caused her some amount of consternation. Germany had been hostile to her as a defenseless young child who posed a threat to precisely no one. It was a very difficult period as she considered what it would mean to her to return to Germany. Eventually, she told herself that the German people had no way of knowing her history. Her last name was now Mac Vittie, not Isaack, and as far as anyone would be concerned, she was an American GI's wife, presumptively an American herself.

So they went to Germany, but Lisa's pregnancy prevented her from flying. At the time, doctors did not want a mother to fly if her pregnancy had any indications of trouble. Since Lisa fit their definition, she took a ship to Germany. The return to Germany was eerily similar to her flight from Germany—an ocean voyage, New York to Le Havre; then a slow train from Le Havre to Paris, where Mac met her and they traveled to Spandahlem, and finally by car to Dudeldorf, where their first home was.

Lisa did not let anyone know she even spoke German until she knew them well, and this worked for her. People treated her like any other American wife, and she was fine with that. It gave her the ability to see that the German people were not the same as the government that had rejected her as a child.

Eventually they moved from Dudeldorf to Speicher. Lisa used her duffel bag from when she was active duty to carry clothes because it fit a lot of clothes into a small space. The side of the bag was, as was all military gear, stenciled with her name. The truck came by, picked up the bag from their house in Dudeldorf, drove it over to Speicher, and dropped it off at the new house. It sat by the side of the road, "ISAACK" stenciled across it. Luckily enough, Lisa had been in Germany long enough that this was merely uncomfortable, and she got the bag inside as soon as possible.

A few days later, her landlady approached her to say, "I wish to tell you something but do not wish to offer offense." Lisa told her she wasn't easily offended and to go ahead. The lady told a tale of the German government paying two men to maintain the Jewish cemetery in town, because all Jewish citizens were removed during Nazi reign, so someone needed to keep the cemetery up. The landlady and her husband walked each evening, and the Jewish cemetery was on their normal route. It seems that one of the gentlemen whom the government had been paying to take care of the cemetery had seen her bag with "ISAACK" printed on the side, and these two men had convinced themselves that the government had sent her to check up on them. They had not been taking care of the cemetery, but for the last three days, they had been out there, working hard to get it into shape. To this day, Lisa chuckles when she thinks of this encounter and feels it is a form of poetic justice.

Lisa's maternal grandparents lived in the British sector of Berlin, and Lisa and Mac were able to visit them during their three years in Germany. Once in 1959, they dropped their oldest daughter, Dawn Wendy, off with the grandparents and fooled their way through Checkpoint Charlie to enter the Russian sector. Lisa's paternal grandparents had lived there, and Lisa and Mac traveled to where the house had been. All that remained of their building was the balcony, stretching up several stories. The rest of the building had collapsed.

Upon their return, they admitted that they had sneaked into the Russian zone to see her other grandparents' house. Her grandparents were livid, and they made certain that the couple understood how foolish that was for a US airman and a former US WAC. Now Lisa is certain that at least part of their concern was because they, in their dotage and having survived the horror of World War II, would have been stuck with Lisa and Mac's young daughter, had they been caught. No doubt some of it was also fear of losing even more of their decimated family.

Stumble Stones are cobblestones, or in some cases plaques placed in the ground, marking where European Jews lived when they were taken by the Nazis. They are placed in the street outside the former residence, and are slightly raised from the surrounding terrain. The relatively new German tradition of Stumble Stones would pay homage to Lisa's paternal grandparents many years later, when Lisa and Fred were invited to Berlin to attend the dedication of the Stumble Stone honoring their loss in the street in front of where that building had stood.

Return to America and Living the Dream

When they returned to the United States, the Mac Vitties were stationed at Wurtsmith Air Force Base in Michigan. Lisa had been a city girl her entire life, but Wurtsmith was at a small town in the country. In spite of the jarring difference, this is where they chose to raise their family. And a family they built, four children: Dawn Wendy, Herbert Walter Jr., Kurt Phillip, and Donald Wilbur. For the next thirty-four years, they lived near Wurtsmith, until their children were grown and for a decade after the last had left home.

When their youngest child entered school, Lisa found a job with the civil service, working in accounting. It was a career she enjoyed and excelled at. While her children were growing up, Lisa decided that a degree was in order. While raising children and working full-time, she attended college and received her degree in accounting. After the last of the children left home, Lisa received an opportunity to go to work as an accountant for the Corps of Engineers in Cincinnati. Lisa and Mac moved there, and she finished her career in public service in Cincinnati, which would be their home thereafter.

Lisa and Mac traveled to China in these years. While there, Lisa was able to visit Shanghai and some of the few buildings that still exist unchanged from the 1940s. She was once again impressed with the welcoming attitude of the people of Shanghai, and she thoroughly enjoyed the trip. Years later, she and her brother Fred returned to Shanghai to donate to the Shanghai Jewish Refugees Museum a photo album of Shanghai in the thirties and early forties that Fred had inherited.

While living in Cincinnati, Lisa also finally discovered the fate of her paternal grandmother. They knew that her paternal grandfather had died during "arrest," if you could call picking up innocent civilians and sending them to prison for the crime of being born Jewish as "arrest." But her grandmother had been a vague story with no definitive end. After being arrested in Berlin, she was shipped to various holding camps in the city and was finally sent by train to the Teresienshtadt concentration camp in the (current) Czech Republic. She was later sent by train to the Minsk concentration camp in Belarus and finally to Maly Trostinec on the outskirts of Minsk. The sole function of Maly Trostinec was an extermination camp. Like everyone else sent there, Lisa's grandmother was "euthanized."

Lisa and her brother Fred went to Germany in 2015 to place the memorial of her grandmother next to her grandfather's grave in a Berlin cemetery, finally offering some closure. During this trip to Germany, she also found a picture of her sister's school class hanging in a Holocaust museum. The museum staff was happy to have information about one of the girls in the picture and gave her a copy of the picture.

Continuing with her belief that she owes America and her fellow Americans something, Lisa gave blood at every safe opportunity until a medical condition made her no longer eligible. She gave many gallons of blood over the years.

FAMILY AND CHILDREN ARE IMPORTANT
So far, Lisa and Mac's family includes four children, fourteen grandchildren, twenty-two great-grandchildren, and five great-great-grandchildren. To Lisa,

this is the real measure of her success. To those descendants, *she* is the real measure of success.

Since retiring from the Corps of Engineers, Lisa has devoted her free time to serving the American Legion and to speaking at elementary schools to children about the Holocaust in general and her experiences in particular. Part of her service with the American Legion includes being a member of the color guard. Lisa insists on carrying the POW/MIA flag when it is used, just one more attempt to honor the American soldiers who fought and died to secure her freedom.

It is Lisa's sincere hope that this recounting will help historians understand the period just a bit more and those going through tough times to understand that it probably isn't forever. And she wants people to understand that you can find joy, if you look for it.

ENDNOTES

i. Hans Von Luck, *Panzer Commander* (Berlin and Paris: Dell Paperbacks, 1991). See chapter 14 in particular. Although highly decorated, then Major von Luck was denied permission to marry a "1/8th Jewess." He maintained his engagement.

ii. See, for example,
> Berl Falbaum, ed., *Shanghai Remembered* (Momentum Books LLC, 2005) and
> Sigmund Tobias, *Strange Haven* (University of Illinois Press, 1999), 4–5.

iii. This is excellently explored in Peter Harmsen, *Shanghai 1937: Stalingrad on the Yangtze* (Casemate Publishers, 2015).

iv. Colleen O'Connor, "From Nazi Terror to Shanghai Squalor," *The Denver Post,* November 21, 2004, 1L, 4L.

v. David Kranzler, *Japanese, Nazis, and Jews: The Jewish Refugee Community of Shanghai, 1938–1945* (Yeshiva University Press, 1976), 282–84.

vi. Best explored in Federick Wakeman Jr., *Policing Shanghai, 1927–1937* (Phillip E. Lilienthal Books, 1995).

vii. "Shanghai International Settlement," Wikipedia. See the "List of Chairmen of the Shanghai Municipal Council."

viii. Kranzler, *Japanese, Nazis, and Jews,* 169–247.

ix. "Baghdadi Jews in Early Shanghai," Malaise J. Meyer, Sino-Judaic Institute, accessed March 13, 2017, http://www.sino-judaic.org/index.php?page=shanghai_history.

x. Kranzler, *Japanese, Nazis, & Jews*, 493–94.

xi. Ibid., 303.

ABOUT THE AUTHOR

Lisa MacVittie delivers talks to middle and high school students about the Holocaust and about her experience as a member of Shanghai's Jewish refugee community. Through her work, she aims to inspire her listeners while educating them to watch for signs of future atrocities.

Donald MacVittie has written in a wide range of genres, among them fantasy, technical manuals, and historical biography. He has a master of science from Nova Southeastern University, and his writing has received an award from the American Society for Business Publication Editors.